SM99003114
12.99.

THE ORGANIZATIONAL LEARNING CYCLE
Second Edition

The Organizational Learning Cycle

How We Can Learn Collectively

Second Edition

Nancy M. Dixon

Gower

First edition published 1994 by McGraw-Hill Book Company.

This edition published by
Gower Publishing Limited
Gower House
Croft Road
Aldershot
Hampshire GU11 3HR
England

Gower
Old Post Road
Brookfield
Vermont 05036
USA

British Library Cataloguing in Publication Data
Dixon, Nancy M., 1937–
    The organizational learning cycle: how we can learn collectively. – 2nd ed.
    1. Communication in organizations   2. Organizational behaviour
    3. Organizational effectiveness
    I. Title
    158.7

ISBN 0 566 08058 3

Library of Congress Cataloging-in-Publication Data
    Dixon, Nancy M., 1937–
        The organizational learning cycle: how we can learn collectively /
    Nancy M. Dixon. – 2nd ed.
        p.   cm.
    Includes bibliographical references and index.
    ISBN 0–566–08058–3
    1. Organizational learning. I. Title.
    HD58.82.D59 1999
    158.7 – dc21   98–30675
                                                                          CIP

Phototypeset in 11 point Palatino by Intype London Ltd and printed in Great Britain at the University Press, Cambridge

This book is dedicated to Reg Revans whose thinking has been so far ahead of his time, that after 50 years, the world is only just catching up.

Contents

List of Figures   xi
Preface   xiii

1 Introduction   1
  The relationship between learning and change   2
  The changing nature of work   4
  Defining organizational learning   6

2 A theoretical framework of individual learning   13
  The difference that makes a difference   15
  Interpreting and organizing data   17
  Learning and truth   27
  Development of meaning structures   28
  Relationship of meaning structures to action   29
  Limitations of working memory   31
  Meta-cognition   37
  The human need to learn   38
  Summary   39

3 **The hallways of learning**   43
   Private meaning   44
   Accessible meaning   46
   Collective meaning   48
   Organizations learn in the hallways   50
   Unpredictable outcomes   57
   Collective meaning versus group decisions   58
   Summary   59

4 **The organizational learning cycle**   63
   Four steps   63
   Chaparral Steel   68
   World Health Organization   76
   Johnsonville Foods   82

5 **A theoretical framework for organizational learning**   93
   Step 1 – Widespread generation of information   93
   Step 2 – Integrating new/local information into
       the organizational context   98
   Step 3 – Collectively interpreting the information   103
   Organizational dialogue   110
   Changing tacit organizational assumptions   116
   Step 4 – Authority to take responsible action
       based on the interpreted meaning   120

6 **Infrastructure for organizational learning**   125
   Quadrant 1 – Configure systems to move
       information across organizational boundaries   128
   Quadrant 2 – Build infrastructure to support
       system-level dialogue   136
   Quadrant 3 – Organize work to disseminate
       decision making for speed and flexibility   141
   Quadrant 4 – Measure results to capture lessons
       learned   146
   Getting started   150

7 **Measuring organizational learning**   155
   Facilitating factors   156

Changes in organizational knowledge 158
New or altered organizational action 162
Organizational outcomes 164
Using measurement for learning 164

8 Developing managers for organizational learning 167
Situating learning in real work 170
Defining a less central role for experts 171
Spaced rather than compressed time frames 173
Learning in community rather than individually 174
No guarantees 176
Illustrations of management development
    programmes 176

**9 The responsibilities of members in an organization
that is learning** 183
Five responsibilities that offer a new way of thinking 187
Sharing in the responsibility for the *governance* of
    the organization 194
Preparing organizational members for their
    responsibilities 196

10 Defining a culture that supports learning 199
The nature of reality and truth 203
The nature of time 205
The nature of human nature 208
The nature of human relationships 210
The relationship of the organization to the
    environment 211
Information and communication 212
Uniformity versus diversity 213
The nature of causality 213
Summary 214

11 Organizational learning and beyond 217

Appendix A: Definitions of organizational learning 227
Appendix B: Glossary 231
Index 235

Figures

1.1	Planned versus continuous change	4
2.1	Development of meaning structures in individuals	17
2.2	An inkblot	18
2.3	Sharon's long-term memory	21
2.4	Introduction of new information into Sharon's current understanding	23
2.5	Integration of new information into Sharon's long-term memory	24
2.6	Revised map of Sharon's long-term memory	25
2.7	Relationship between knowledge and action	30
2.8	Kolb's experiential learning cycle	40
3.1	Three types of meaning structure	44
3.2	Organizational meaning structures	46
3.3	Development of hallways	51
4.1	The organizational learning cycle	64
4.2	The organizational learning cycle and the experiential learning cycle	65
4.3	The organizational learning cycle for Chaparral Steel	75
4.4	The organizational learning cycle for WHO	81

4.5	The organizational learning cycle for Johnsonville Foods	89
5.1	Elements in the organizational learning cycle	94
5.2	Argyris' framework for a theory of action	117
5.3	Framework for an organizational causal map	118
5.4	Organizational causal map – low productivity	119
5.5	Organizational causal map – budget	119
6.1	Infrastructure to support organizational learning	127
6.2	Quadrant 1 of the infrastructure	129
6.3	Quadrant 2 of the infrastructure	137
6.4	Quadrant 3 of the infrastructure	141
6.5	Quadrant 4 of the infrastructure	147
7.1	Causal relationships assumed in measuring organizational learning	157
10.1	Organizational assumptions that facilitate organizational learning	204

Preface

In writing this book, I have drawn heavily on the literature of organizational learning, much of which has been in existence for twenty-five years, and in some cases even longer. I also draw on recent concepts from the fields of social cognition and adult development, as well as understandings from organizational and cognitive psychology. I bring in ideas from the closely related topic of knowledge management. These ideas are framed within my own concept of organizational learning.

There are two theorists who have so profoundly influenced my own thinking that I am no longer able to distinguish my ideas from theirs: Reg Revans and Chris Argyris. Fifty years ago, Revans developed the original ideas of action learning. His fundamental belief that 'there is no learning without action and no responsible action without learning' has influenced my writing, my interventions with organizations and my university teaching. The basic values of Argyris, which are valid information, free and informed choice, and vigilant monitoring of the implementation of those choices, have influenced my work with organizations, the way I conduct research, and most significantly how I regard basic human interaction. I have attempted to give credit to both of these theorists when I draw directly upon their writing, but I recognize that their influence colours much of what I have written here in ways I may not even be aware of. Their influence is clearly evidenced in the four major themes of the book:

1   Learning is a part of work and work involves learning; these are not separate functions but intertwined; the separation we have made of them is artificial and often does not serve us well.
2   Learning is not only or even primarily about obtaining correct information or answers from knowledgeable others; it is fundamentally about making meaning out of the experience we and others have in the world.
3   Organizational learning results from intentional and planned efforts to learn. Although it can and does occur accidentally, organizations cannot afford to rely on learning through chance.
4   As a collective we are capable of learning our way to the answers we need to address our difficult problems. It is ourselves we must rely on for these answers rather than experts, who can, at best, only provide us with answers that have worked in the past.

I view organizations as purposeful social systems which have three interrelated tasks: (1) the development of the organization itself, (2) the development of the individuals who comprise the organization, and (3) the development of the larger system of which the organization is a part – the community, nation, and planet (Ackoff, 1981). I have undertaken this book because I have an abiding belief in the power of collective learning to address these three tasks with far greater success than they have previously been addressed.

It is the first of these three tasks which organizations have taken as their primary focus: trying to make the organization more productive and competitive. We have only recently come to comprehend the nested nature of systems well enough to consider that the development of the organization cannot be divorced from the development of those who comprise its sub-systems and the supra-systems in which it is embedded.

In maintaining this unitary and limited focus, we have slighted the development of individuals and remained unresponsive to the common good. When we have attended to these, we have treated them as 'in service of' rather than 'in relationship to' the organization. We have, for example, concerned ourselves with the development of individuals only to the extent that development will make the organization more productive. We have focused on the larger system only to the extent that we are required to legally or that is necessary in order to ward off negative publicity.

Even the efforts we have expended on the first of these tasks, as considerable as they have been, have had little to do with development. Our efforts have often seemed more like persuasion or even at times manipulation. We seem to equate development with trying to make the organization comply with our latest theory. So clumsy are our efforts that, by analogy, if the organization were a budding flower, our development effort would equate to tugging and pulling at the petals with the intent of forcing its growth. We have made little use of the collective reasoning and intelligence of the organization in this development effort. But the collective is capable of changing itself into something new and choiceful if we use learning rather than intimidation as the mechanism for development.

In this book I am trying to clarify organizational learning well enough to assist organizations in developing in ways that do service to and are interrelated with the other two systems. The term development is familiar from its use in 'management development' and 'employee development' programmes which strive to develop skills and competencies that are useful in carrying out the organization's strategy. I am, however, using the term in the much fuller sense of the development of the human being. Organizations have put considerable resources into management development, but it is human development that I fear we have badly neglected.

Human development does not stop at the beginning of adulthood; it continues throughout the lifetime of the individual. As human beings we are continually influenced and shaped by the world in which we function. We each have the potential to develop 'a more inclusive, differentiated, permeable, and integrated perspective' (Mezirow, 1991, p. 155). But we also have the possibility of becoming increasingly closed, disillusioned, and fragmented. To develop, that is, to change in the direction of our potential, we must function within an environment that fosters, or at least permits, such development. Organizations, by and large, do not. In recent years we have seen large numbers of employees dropping out of organizations because they recognize that their own development is in jeopardy. This exodus has been particularly true for women, whose sensitivity to development issues may be heightened by their more recent entry into many parts of organizations. But men as well have begun to recognize that they must make developmental choices that, in many cases, remove them from traditional organizations.

We have created organizations that are often detrimental to the human beings that work in them. Our organizations often engender alienation in employees, inhibit human development and encourage dishonesty and distrust between ourselves and others. I am not speaking only of for-profit corporations, but also of universities, where much of my working life has been spent, not-for-profit organizations and government agencies. With few exceptions, the organizations we have created operate in ways that are antithetical to the work environment that we would choose for ourselves or that we understand to result in healthy adult development.

It is unlikely that organizational members will become more integrated while denying meaningful parts of who they are; unlikely that they will become more permeable (open) while daily hiding what they are doing. As adults we spend most of our lives in organizations, certainly most of our waking hours. If we are to continue to develop, it will happen at work; if it cannot happen there, it will probably not happen. It is ironic that the amazing capability of the human mind has created complex organizations that in turn stifle the growth and well-being of those that created them.

The examples of our developmental distress are numerous

and familiar. All of us in organizations find ourselves taking actions which we know will not work, while pretending that we are making a good faith effort. We play games with budgets, deliberately padding them, while claiming we need every penny. We deceive others, not out of perversity, but because it is the only way we can find to get our jobs done. We often feel we are being treated like children, particularly when others withhold information or make decisions for 'our own good'; and we, as well, withhold information from others for 'their good'. Such actions have become part of our taken-for-granted assumptions about how we must function in organizations in order to survive and get ahead. We have come to believe that this is 'just the way it is', 'all organizations have politics', 'you just have to play the game'.

Jerry Harvey (1989) created a clever true/false instrument, 'The Phrog Index', that reveals to the respondent some of his or her own debilitating taken-for-granted assumptions. He first elicits a response from us on what we believe about how people in general must function in organizations in order to get the job done. Then he turns the questions back on us to reveal the inconsistency of our response. A few items from the Phrog Index illustrate this point:

- Occasionally, it is necessary for a manager to lie   T F
  to or deceive others in his/her own organization
  in order to achieve organizational objectives.
- I work most effectively with those who   T F
  occasionally lie to me.
- It is important that a manager be objective when   T F
  dealing with subordinates on matters such as
  performance appraisal, pay, promotion, and recognition.
- I work most effectively with those who treat me as   T F
  an object.

If we want organizations to become systems which are able to learn and transform themselves, then these organizations will have to be comprised of subsystems, individuals, who have been enabled to develop more inclusive, integrated and differentiated perspectives. Likewise, if we want individuals to develop in these ways, we will have to construct organizations that foster that development. One begets the other.

The lack of focus on the development of the larger system, of which each organization is a subsystem, is as disquieting an issue as is the suppression of individual development. That larger system includes the community, nation and environment.

Bellah et al. (1985) note that initially the term corporation implied an organization to whom the government granted special status because it clearly served the public interest. They advocate reasserting the idea 'that incorporation is a concession of public authority to a private group in return for service to the public good'. In their opinion such a change would alter 'what is now called the "social responsibility of the corporation" from its present status, where it is often a kind of public relations whipped cream decorating the corporate pudding, to a constitutive structural element in the corporation itself' (p. 290). They say, 'Management would become a profession in the older sense of the word, involving not merely standards of technical competence but standards of public obligation that could at moments of conflict override obligations to the corporate employer' (p. 290).

This conception of what an organization is or could be is far from the way most organizations currently function in relation to the larger system. Many of our organizations, for example, knowingly sell products that are harmful to other human beings, or act in ways that damage the environment. Many of our organizations buy companies only to break them up and sell off the parts. Many do not pay a fair share of taxes. Many overcharge their governments for products and service.

I am not suggesting that we, as representatives of our organizations, intend harm when we act in such ways, but that our actions are mediated by our taken-for-granted assumptions about organizations that are based for the most part on a mechanical analogy. We view the organization as a kind of machine whose purpose is to serve the ends of the owners or stockholders, while employees are seen as parts of the mechanism that need to be allocated and controlled in order to achieve the owners' ends. If, instead of the mechanical analogy, we were to fully embrace an analogy of the organization as a purposeful social system, we would derive a very different set of actions – a set that fosters learning.

While acknowledging that it is our taken-for-granted assumptions that guide our actions, rather than some sinister intent, we are nevertheless jointly responsible for the organizations we have created. Top management of any organization bears some responsibility, but so does each and every organizational member who colludes through silence or through the acceptance of their own powerlessness. The resolution of these difficulties we have created is also a joint responsibility.

Through collective learning we have the possibility of transforming the organizations we have created, not instantaneously nor without considerable struggle, but in the direction that we choose. Learning is the most potent force for change that exists. It was William James who said, 'The greatest discovery in our generation is that human beings, by changing the inner attitudes of their minds can change the outer aspects of their lives'. Learning, as I will use the term in this book, goes beyond the acquisition of existing knowledge.

It is an approach to human functioning that emphasizes the intention to 'make sense of' our world and to act responsibly upon the understanding we derive from that sense-making. Understanding without action is impotence, and action without understanding is foolish. I am not suggesting that we, as individuals, can change our organizations. I have fallen on my own sword too many times to hold such a belief. It is the learning of the collective that, for me, holds this possibility – what Bohm (1990) calls social intelligence. That intelligence is at the heart of democracy and self-governance. Jefferson said, 'I know of no safe depository of the ultimate powers of the society but the people themselves, and if we think them not enlightened enough to exercise their control with a wholesome discretion, the remedy is not to take it from them, but to inform their discretion'. The truism that a percentage of our workforce does not want the responsibility of self-governance, while it may be accurate, does not relieve them or us of the responsibility to learn, that is to 'make sense of' our world and to act responsibly upon the understanding we derive from that sense-making.

As a global society we have been learning, slowly and falteringly – the Berlin wall fell, the totalitarian government of the Soviet Union gave way. We are learning together that we must act to save the planet, that we must eliminate nuclear weapons, that we must recycle our waste. It is extremely difficult for a global society, with all of its diversity, to learn. It is difficult for nations to learn; yet they can and do learn. South Africa is learning about its own injustice; the USA is learning about how to conserve rather than exploit its environment. Organizations can learn as well. And if we can get better at collective learning at the organizational level we may be able to use that understanding to increase our ability to learn at the national and societal level.

Learning is the most magnificent gift we have as human beings. It is a gift we have customarily thought of as an individual capability. Framing learning in that way, we have used our minds to do great things – create glorious music and art, write wonderful books, develop incredible technology, build intricate theories that explain the whole of the universe, and much more.

When we reframe learning as a collective and also as an individual capability, we amplify its power. With such power we might be able to address some of the social issues that are so pervasive and troublesome. We are not without tangible evidence of the power of collective learning. At the micro level the research on learning demonstrates its potency. At the macro level we have the hopeful worldwide trends toward democracy, conservation, health and unity.

Over the past four years, since the publication of the first edition of this book, the idea of organizational learning has found great acceptance in organizations across the US, Great Britain, Europe, Australia and the Netherlands. There are now thousands of organizations, both profit and not-for-profit, that refer to themselves, with considerable pride, as 'learning organizations'. The idea of organizational learning seems to have an intuitive appeal. Organizational members are quite ready to accept that learning and its resultant knowledge is crucial to their continued success and advancement. They want to see themselves, and to be seen by others, as an organization that is learning and is therefore moving forward.

However, organizational learning may serve more as an 'ideal' than an actuality for many of these organizations. It is something they aspire to, but have not yet figured out how to put into place beyond an increased emphasis on training and perhaps renewed efforts to create more open communication. As with many ideals, even very attractive ones, 'the devil is in the details'. So in this second edition I have tried to provide some of the details that I have seen in those organizations that are finding practical ways to implement organizational learning.

To make use of collective knowledge we need to understand it better. It is my hope that this book will make a contribution to that effort – knowledge about how and why collective learning works. A part of that understanding is the way collective learning is related to individual learning. In much of the literature they are treated as two separate phenomena, related only by analogy. This book tries to explicate that relationship.

Chapter 1 considers why organizational learning has caught our attention at this time. I suggest two main factors that necessitate the emphasis on collective rather than individual learning: the changing nature of work that is a result of the dawning Knowledge Age, and the increasing pace of change which often invalidates known answers and demands that we continually learn. In this chapter I operationally define organizational learning and outline the major implementation constructs that are implied in the definition.

Chapters 2, 3 and 4 address some of the difficult questions that organizational learning raises. Who learns? By what process does the learning occur? Does an organization have a mind with which it learns? Is organizational learning simply a heuristic or is it an accurate description of a social system? I start from the position that organizational learning is an extrapolation of the concept of individual learning. Thus, any model of organizational learning must be based in, and be compatible with, individual learning theory. To build this relationship I articulate a theory of individual learning in Chapter 2 and take that a step further in Chapter 3.

Chapter 4 describes an organizational learning cycle. Three case examples, Chaparral Steel, The World Health Organization and Johnsonville Foods, illustrate the cycle.

Chapter 5 describes the organizational learning cycle in greater depth, adding examples from other organizations. Here I provide theory and research data to support the organizational learning cycle.

Chapter 6 uses the poles of the organizational learning cycle to form four quadrants through which I describe the infrastructure that is needed to make the theory of organizational learning a reality in organizations. This chapter pulls in concepts from knowledge management and gives examples of technological and face-to-face processes that facilitate the growth and sharing of knowledge within an organization.

Chapter 7 is about the use of measurement in organizations. Here I advocate that although measurement can be of little help in proving that organizational learning is impacting the bottom line, it nevertheless has an important role to play in collective learning.

Chapter 8 talks about the need to change the way we develop managers if we want development programmes to be compatible with, indeed to support, organizational learning. This chapter may be of particular interest to human resource professionals who are charged with the task of designing learning experiences for managers.

Chapter 9 describes the responsibilities of organizational members in an organization that is learning. It advocates that organizational members have both the right and the responsibility to help create the organizations in which they function.

Chapter 10 describes the culture that promotes organizational learning. I have framed this discussion around many of the basic organizational assumptions suggested by Schein (1992).

Chapter 11 draws together the relationship between organizational learning and the democratization of organizations. I have talked about why and how organizational learning leads not only to greater participation, but to the more democratic idea of shared authority.

There are two appendices. Appendix A is a compilation of definitions of organizational learning drawn from the literature. I note the main similarities and differences across the definitions. Appendix B is a glossary of terms, most of them introduced in Chapters 2 and 3. I started writing this book with the firm intent to keep technical terms and certainly jargon to a minimum. Having completed it and contemplated the need for a glossary, I discover I have come nowhere near reaching that goal. The difficulty I found, and which the reader may find as well, is that the term 'learning' has so many meanings that to talk with any clarity about different aspects of learning I have needed to use differing terms, otherwise the whole thing becomes a great muddle. It is necessary, for instance, to differentiate the act of learning from the results of learning. The term 'learning' in common usage implies both things. I offer apologies in advance to the reader and hope the glossary will be of some help in wading through the terms.

Finally, I give my thanks to colleagues who reviewed drafts of the first edition of the book: Mike Pedler, John Burgoyne, George Roth, Alan Mumford, Ed Blankenhagen and Marty Castleberg, and the second edition: Doris Adams, Rick Ross and Art Kleiner.

I have been warmed and pleased by the response to the first edition of *The Organizational Learning Cycle*. The many people that have called me, sent e-mail messages, written reviews, and talked about the ways they have been able to make use of the ideas in that book has been very gratifying. In this business of writing, it seems you spend an eternity just getting the words down on paper, followed by a very long delay while the publisher and printer 'do their thing'. Then, when you have almost forgotten that you wrote anything, there comes a call from someone to talk about the ideas in the book that you experience as a delightful surprise. It is the opportunity to exchange ideas with colleagues, both new and old, that makes it all very worth while.

References

Ackoff, R. L. (1981). *Creating the Corporate Future*. New York: John Wiley & Sons.

Bellah, R.N., Madsen, R., Sulivan, W., Swidler, A. and Tipton, S.M. (1985). *Habits of the Heart*. Berkeley: University of California Press.

Bohm, D. (1990). 'On Dialogue' (transcript). Ojai CA: David Bohm Seminars.

Harvey, J. (1989). *Phrog Index* (unpublished). The George Washington University.

Mezirow, J. (1991). *Transformative Dimensions of Adult Learning*. San Francisco: Jossey-Bass.

Schein, E. H. (1992). *Organizational Culture and Leadership* (2nd edn.). San Francisco: Jossey-Bass.

1 Introduction

We have entered the Knowledge Age, and the new currency is learning. It is learning, not knowledge itself, which is critical. Knowledge is the result of learning and is ephemeral, constantly needing to be revised and updated. Learning is 'sense making': it is the process that leads to knowledge. Thurber once said, 'In times of change learners shall inherit the earth, while the learned are beautifully equipped for a world that no longer exists'. Organizational learning requires learning rather than being learned.

Unfortunately, the term 'learning', perhaps because of early school experiences, for most of us has come to mean to 'thoroughly grasp what an expert knows'. For example, when we want to 'learn about' quality we study the processes that someone far more knowledgeable than ourselves, such as Deming, Juran or Crosby, has devised. If we want to 'learn' how to lead, we turn to Bennis, DePree or Blanchard to learn how the experts suggest we lead. We may modify the expert's processes to fit our own situation, but when we talk about learning we are essentially talking about finding and comprehending someone else's *answer*. The premises of this conception of learning are that:

1   There is a right answer.
2   The answer is known.
3   If we can identify the 'knower' and comprehend those ideas, we can apply the answer to achieve our goals.

These are not false premises, but they are limited ones, useful with some types of issues, but inappropriate for others. These premises are most useful when the answers are known and when the problems are stable. The caveat is that for most of the problems that organizations face there are no known answers: they are problems that have never before been experienced, and those problems exist within a context of great turbulence, so that even if we had answers that had worked before, it is not clear that they would fit our changed situation.

Organizational learning is based on a very different set of premises:

1   There are many right answers, as in the concept of equifinality; there are many ways to reach the same goal.
2   People who are concerned about and affected by a problem are capable of developing useful knowledge to resolve it.
3   Learning occurs in a context of work and praxis, and results from intentional effort.

The relationship between learning and change

A formula borrowed from ecology states that in order for an organism to survive, its rate of learning must be equal to or greater than the rate of change in its environment. The formula is written $L \geq C$. Considering organizations as organisms, it is apparent that organizations are going to have to increase their rate of learning to survive in these times of unprecedented change.

The formula, however, does not acknowledge our human ability to change the environment as well as adapt to it. It is commonly held that change is caused by forces over which organizations have little control. However, the reality is that we create much of the change to which we must then adapt – for example, we create technological change, alter gender relations and create multinational organizations. We are unique, of all creatures on the face of the earth, in that we can not only respond to, but also alter, our environment (Botkin et al., 1979).

Not only can we physically change our environment, we can alter it by reframing or reconceptualizing it. Weick (1979) uses the term 'enactment' to indicate the reciprocal influence between organizations and their environment. In part, the concept of enactment implies a self-fulfilling prophecy: the perceiver tends to see what is expected. But the concept of enactment goes further, to suggest that the organization implants meaning on the mass of data available and thereby creates the environment in which it will function.

Knowledge that we create through learning allows us to change our environment, whether by reframing it, physically altering it or both. The two factors, learning and change, reinforce each other. The faster the rate of change the more new knowledge we must create to deal with the change; the more knowledge we create the faster we change our world. Friedlander (1983) says, 'Learning is the process that underlies and gives birth to change. Change is the child of learning' (p. 194).

It is certainly possible for change to occur without being preceded by learning. A hurricane, a hostile takeover or new government regulations can all necessitate organizational change. When such change occurs it is followed by organizational learning, even when it was not preceded by it.

Change is preceded by organizational learning when, for example, an organization learns from its customers that product change is needed; it comes to understand that its reward structure is not effective; or it envisions a desired future toward which it chooses to strive. Organizational learning can lead to change which can lead to more organizational learning.

Organizational learning then, can lead to the continuous

transformation of an organization and its environment. However, that transformation is not the familiar one-step process of moving from state A, which has been deemed insufficient, to state B, the better way. Organizational learning does not define an end state, but rather is the process that allows the organization to continually generate new states, as in A to B to C to D, and so on. No organizational problem stays solved for long, because each solution engenders a new problem. The key to organizational learning is not only the ability of the organization to transform itself and its environment, but to do so continuously (see Figure 1.1).

Planned change   A ─────→ B

Change through learning   A ─→ B ─→ C ─→ D ─→

Figure 1.1   Planned versus continuous change

The changing nature of work

Whether the Knowledge Age began with the popularization of the personal computer, as Zuboff (1988) would have it, or with the creation of the GI Bill (that sent returning soldiers back to universities), as Drucker (1992) assumes, it is certain that it is here. In the 1990s, to work in an organization is more likely to mean manipulating information than raw materials. The vast majority of jobs require individuals to interpret, analyse, and/ or synthesize information. Where in the past such requirements were asked only of high-level managers, they are now demanded of workers at all levels. The terms 'interpretation', 'analysis' and 'synthesis' are often used as synonyms for learning; thus learning and work have become synonymous terms. 'As noted by Howell and Cooke (1989; in Goldstein and Gilliam 1990), smart machines increase the cognitive complexity of the tasks performed by the human being. Instead of simple procedural and predictable tasks, the human becomes responsible for inferences, diagnoses, judgment, and decision making, often under severe time pressure' (Goldstein and Gilliam, 1990, p. 139). Rather than learn in preparation for work, *employees must learn their way out of the work problems they address.*

The role of the person who supervises such ambiguous work has also changed; managers can no longer rely on control, but must find leverage in jointly establishing direction and goals. Learning creates equals, not subordinates, and thus work is increasingly conceived as a team effort. In past decades it was possible to teach workers how to do a specific task and then set them to doing it. Managers were responsible for making sure the workers were following the procedure they had been taught, a control task. It is, however, not possible for managers to provide such specific instruction for the task of interpreting, synthesizing and analysing information. Rules, to the extent they can be provided at all, are more useful as a heuristic that offers guidance but cannot provide answers. In this sense, knowledge workers more closely resemble the self-employed than they do a conventional workforce (Drucker, 1992).

Perelman (1984) notes: 'By the beginning of the next century, three quarters of the jobs in the U.S. economy will involve creating and processing knowledge. Knowledge workers will find that continual learning is not only a prerequisite of employment but is a major form of work' (p. xvii). Zuboff (1988), in her book *In the Age of the Smart Machine*, explains that information technology has altered basic assumptions about the relationship between work and learning. She says:

Learning is no longer a separate activity that occurs either before one enters the workplace or in remote classroom settings. Nor is it an activity preserved for a managerial group. The behaviors that define learning and the behaviors that define being productive are one and the same. Learning is not something that requires time out from being engaged in productive activity; learning is the heart of productive activity. To put it simply, learning is the new form of labor. (p. 395)

It is customary to think of learning and work as being separate activities, the former preceding the latter. Zuboff suggests that more often learning is the work task. Zuboff considers 'intellective skills', which are the ability to make meaning and exercise critical judgement, as the organization's most precious resource. The organization's investment in upgrading and maintaining those skills is comparable with that of investing in technology itself.

It is the recognition of these two factors, the changing nature of work and the increased rate of change itself, that prompts organizations to view learning as a more critical variable than it might have been in the past. Organizations are trying to figure out how to improve their processes, transfer best practices from one part of the organization to another, more quickly incorporate new technologies, make collective use of what their subsystems know – all learning tasks.

Defining organizational learning

For the purposes of this book I shall define organizational learning as 'the intentional use of learning processes at the individual, group and system level to continuously transform the organization in a direction that is increasingly satisfying to its stakeholders'.

The complexity of this definition suggests some need for decoding. The definition begins with the term 'intentional'. All organizations learn to a greater or lesser extent; they adapt to environmental constraints, prevent the repetition of past mistakes and generate innovative, new ideas. Although such organizational learning examples occur, equally typical are situations in which learning is not achieved, that is, organizations repeat their mistakes, fail to adapt to customer needs, and are unable to improve their processes to meet rising competitive standards. Even when organizational learning does occur, it is often accidental rather than as the result of intention. Lacking intentional processes at the individual, group and system levels to facilitate organizational learning, most organizations are inefficient learners and much that could be learned is lost or missed.

In common usage the term 'learning' has two related but very different meanings. It is often used as a noun, as in 'What did you learn from your experience?' Its meaning in this context could be equated with knowledge, that is, the result of an effort of comprehension. At the collective level, in using the term in the context of knowledge, we might ask 'What has the organization learned from past experiences?'

The second way the term 'learning' is used is as a verb, as in 'to learn'. Here the reference is to processes, as in 'She is a good learner' or 'I am learning a new word-processing program'. At the collective level we might use the term 'learning' as a process to ask, 'What do we need to do to be able to correct our mistakes as we go along?' or 'How might we go about understanding this better?' In the definition provided above, and indeed throughout the book, I am using the term in the latter sense rather than the former. Organizational learning, as I am using the term, is the processes the organization employs to gain new understanding or to correct the current understanding; it is not the accumulated knowledge of the organization. This is a nontrivial differentiation from my perspective. A main premise of this book is that learning is the construction and reconstruction of meaning and as such it is a dynamic process. Accumulated knowledge, then, is of less significance than are the processes needed to continuously revise or create knowledge. Those processes can be viewed as a cycle that starts with (1) the widespread generation of information, (2) integrates the new information into the organizational context, (3) collectively interprets the information and (4) then authorizes organizational members to take responsible action based on the interpreted meaning. The fourth step then feeds into the first to generate new information.

The first step includes the process through which the organization acquires information, including whose responsibility it is, and the diversity of the sources of information from which it is gained. This step also involves building learning processes into any organizational action or event so that organizational members learn through it as well as accomplish it. It implies experimentation and self-correction. The second step deals with the speed, accuracy and extent of the dissemination of information; who receives what information and when. The third step comprises the processes that are in place to facilitate organizational members interpreting information. Receiving information and making sense of it are very different processes. Learning has not occurred until organizational members make sense of the information. Because organizational learning involves collective rather than only individual interpretation, that process cannot be left to chance, but requires organized processes. Finally, when organizational members work to make sense of information they need the authorization to act on that understanding. This step implies local rather than centralized control.

Organizational learning requires all four steps of the organizational learning cycle. It is not sufficient to focus on only one of the two steps, because any one without the others is ineffective. For example, if organizational members collectively interpret a situation but their learning is not informed by accurate information, the learning is ineffective. Likewise, if organizational members learn ways to improve their organizational actions but are unable to put their new understandings to use, the learning itself is wasted.

The purpose of the organizational learning cycle is the *continuous transformation* of the organization. Earlier I differentiated continuous transformation (A to B to C to D) from change as a one-step event (A to B). The learning processes that are useful in furthering continuous transformation are considerably different from those needed to create a specific change. For the latter the need is to be able to articulate the desired new state, to identify the gaps between the desired and current states and to define steps to close the gap. For continuous change the focus is on the processes that inform and facilitate ongoing change: on the process rather than the destination, recognizing that the destination is only one stop on a longer journey.

To define the term 'organization' I rely on Argyris and Schon (1978). They begin their book, entitled *Organizational Learning*, by asking, 'What is an organization that it can learn?' They explain that a group of people becomes an organization when the individuals which comprise it develop procedures for:

1 Making decisions in the name of the collective.
2 Delegating to individuals the authority to act for the collective.
3 Setting boundaries between the collective and the rest of the world.

By contrast, they depict a mob as a collective of people which may run about and shout but cannot make a decision or take an action in its own name. Until rules or procedures are in place, each individual can act for him- or herself but cannot act in the name of the collective, cannot say 'We have decided'. For the collective to act, members must have an identified vehicle for collective decision making and action. When members have created such rules and procedures they can be said to have organized.

A collective comes together to form an organization in order to accomplish a complex task, one which is too complex for any one individual to accomplish. The organization defines a strategy for decomposing that complex task into simpler components which are regularly delegated to individuals (e.g. president, computer programmer, welder). The organization's task system is a pattern of interconnected roles which is both a design for work and a division of labour. The task system operates through a set of norms, strategies and assumptions which specify how the work gets divided and how the tasks get performed. Such norms, strategies and assumptions include what an acceptable margin of profit is, ways in which communication occurs, who gets promoted, what market to target and how resources are allocated. Although these norms, strategies, and assumptions, perhaps even more than the rules for deciding and acting, may be tacit rather than explicit, they nevertheless guide the way the organization accomplishes its tasks (Argyris and Schon, 1978).

The final part of the definition states 'in a direction that is increasingly satisfying to its stakeholders'. The implication here is a political one – referencing who defines the ends for which the organization strives as well as who defines the means to reach those ends. I am arguing that when information is widely shared and when organizational members use 'intellective skills' and are encouraged to challenge the organization's assumptions, they will also question the ends toward which the organization is striving and will insist upon a shared responsibility in their definition. Moreover, I am suggesting that it is not only organizational members but all of the stakeholders of an organization who must be considered in defining those ends.

The argument that I make in this book is that by employing the processes of the organizational learning cycle organizations can transform themselves. Moreover, the act of organizational learning carries with it a kind of emancipation from hierarchically controlled organizations and engenders greater self-governance and responsibility.

References

Argyris, C. and Schon, D. A. (1978). *Organizational Learning: A Theory of Action Perspective*. Reading MA: Addison-Wesley.

Botkin, J., Elmandjra, M. and Malitza, M. (1979). *No Limits to Learning*. Elmsford, NY: Pergamon Press.

Drucker, P. F. (1992). 'The new society of organizations'. *Harvard Business Review*, September/October, 95–104.

Friedlander, F. (1983). 'Patterns of Individual and Organizational Learning' in Srivastva, Suresh and Associates, *The Executive Mind, New Insights on Managerial Thought and Action*, pp. 192–220. San Francisco: Jossey-Bass Inc.

Goldstein, I. L. and Gilliam, P. C. (1990). 'Training System Issues in the Year 2000'. *American Psychologist*, (45) 2, 134–143.

Perelman, L. (1984). *The Learning Enterprise: Adult Learning, Human Capital and Economic Development*. Washington DC: The Council of State Planning Agencies.

Weick, K. E. (1979). *The Social Psychology of Organizing*. New York: Random House.

Zuboff, S. (1988). *In the Age of the Smart Machine*. New York: Basic Books.

2 A theoretical framework of individual learning

Understanding how we as individuals make sense of the world is at the core of our understanding of how the collective learns. The processes we design for organizational learning must take into account the immense capability as well as the peculiar limitations of individual learning. For example, later in this chapter I shall describe the sizeable amount of individual learning that is tacit. If, in designing ways that subsystems of the organization can learn best practices from each other, we ignore the tacit aspects of learning, we shall construct ineffective processes. Likewise, if we misconceive of individual learning as the passive receipt of information, we might not design into the task of teams the necessary procedures that would allow them to self-correct.

In this chapter I go into considerable detail about how individual learning occurs. I outline how we take in data, how we make meaning of it, and the configuration in which cognitive psychologists postulate that it is stored. I talk about some of the surprising foibles of the human mind – those that get us into trouble but which are paradoxically our greatest strength. I discuss the relationship between what we 'know' and what we think of as truth as well as the relationship between what we know and how we act. I look at meta-cognition, our active monitoring of our learning processes, and finally I discuss the relationship between learning and development.

The extensive detail in this chapter is in part because learning is a complex topic that requires substantial explication if it is to be useful to us in understanding collective learning. But I must confess that my own fascination with learning is equally to blame for the length of the chapter. It is, I find, the most human of capabilities. Perry (1970) says that what an organism does is organize; and what a human organism organizes is meaning. I marvel at what we, as the human race, have been able to achieve because we are such good learners, and I marvel at how easily we are blinded by constructions of our own making. William Blake said it most eloquently:

> I wander thro' each charter'd street
> Near where the charter'd Thames does flow,
> And mark in every face I meet
> Marks of weakness, marks of woe.
>
> In every cry of every Man
> In every Infant's cry of fear,
> In every voice, in every ban,
> The mind-forg'd manacles I hear
>
> *London*

The theory that is discussed in this chapter is based on a constructionist's view of cognition, one of several individual learning theories that I could have employed in such an explanation. A constructionist view of learning starts from the position that learning is the act of interpreting experience, that interpretation is unique to each individual and is both enabled and constrained by the individual's process of sense making. In this chapter I have relied heavily on the ideas of Robert Gagné and Gregory Bateson. The ideas of Chris Argyris have been incorporated as well. Although not generally thought of as a learning theorist, Argyris' work is in agreement with cognitive constructionist theories of learning and, moreover, his work has focused on the intersection between individual and organizational learning.

For many of us the term 'learning' is associated with school or with studying for a difficult test. In this chapter I address learning in a much broader sense, because only a small part of what we, as individuals, 'know' is learned in a school setting. As an example, when McCall et al. (1988) investigated how executives learned what they knew about managing, the executives attributed less than 5 per cent to classroom instruction. If we are to use the concept of individual learning to help us understand organizational learning, we will have to address learning in its broadest sense: that which occurs through our everyday experience.

The difference that makes a difference

There are three ways that we as individuals come to know something:

1 Direct experience (the receipt of sensory data such as colour, sound and pain).
2 Verbal transmission of information (ideas voiced by others, reports, books, formulas etc.).
3 The reorganizing of what we already know into a new configuration.

Differentiating between direct experience, verbal transmission and reorganization of existing meaning does not imply that the process of learning associated with each is separated in time or space. In fact, most learning involves all three simultaneously. For example, as we listen to the explanation of a concept that a colleague offers, we also make inferences based on the intensity with which the individual speaks as well as the accompanying facial and hand gestures.

As human beings we take in only a small part of the information that exists in the world around us. Therefore we cannot lay claim to creating an accurate reproduction of the world in our own minds. Our human sensory equipment is, for example, limited both in terms of the range of sound and the range of light waves that it can perceive; humans cannot see X-rays nor hear a whistle pitched for the ears of a dog. Much of what goes on in the world goes unheeded and unnoticed by us as human beings: it is too small or too vast, too high or too low, too fast or too slow.

Even that class of data which our limited sensory equipment is capable of registering is filtered through our selective attention, which causes us to focus on certain data and to ignore others. For example, we ignore background noise in a movie, we fail to notice who is sitting in most of the cars that are passing us on the highway, and we do not notice what others in the restaurant are wearing. That attention involves a selection process does not imply that it is always intentional selection. Selection is, in fact, most often not under our conscious control. Our sensory receptors appear to be constructed so as to automatically attend to changes in level of intensity that would indicate new data are in the environment: for example, a change in volume, or the movement of an object. It is 'differences' that draw our attention and that are registered by our sensory receptors (see Figure 2.1).

In a conceptual sense, as well, learning is about differences. We attend to that which is different from our current understanding and from our expectations: for example, we notice a friend's behaviour that has changed or that is outside the norm of what we consider acceptable behaviour, or we notice an attitude that a new acquaintance holds that differs markedly from our own. We give attention to a goal that we fell short of reaching. Difference may be produced internally, as in two conflicting ideas we hold, or it may occur between ourselves and the environment (in which I include others). The absence as well as the presence of something can represent difference to us – a letter that was not received or food which is unavailable are differences we notice. However, to learn from difference, we must internalize it. A whistle that is at a pitch too high for us

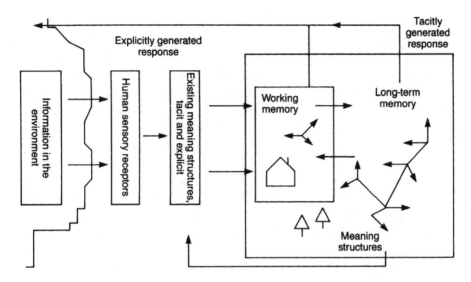

Figure 2.1　Development of meaning structures in individuals

to hear does not represent a difference between silence and the whistle. The proverbial frog, who willingly sat in the pot of water that gradually came to a boil, did not internalize the difference in temperature, except in the most literal sense. 'Information' as Gregory Bateson (1979) says, 'consists of differences that make a difference' (p. 105). To learn we must be able to hold the difference within our minds long enough to make sense of it.

Interpreting and organizing data

We create 'meaning structures' from the data that we encounter in our interaction in the world. Meaning structures are ways we organize data in order to make sense of it. Developing meaning structures is a function of seeing relationships in data, such as what is larger or smaller, what is similar to something else, what belongs to the same category, what cause produces what effect, and what comes first, second and third in a sequence.

The word 'data' as I have used it here could leave the mistaken impression that a bit of reality (data) exists in the external world which we perceive, take in and then categorize. However, I intend quite a different meaning. We do not record data that are in the environment, but rather we receive sensory impressions of a subset of the data and then interpret those sensory impressions. It is out of this interpretation that we create meaning structures.

A useful analogy is an inkblot. An inkblot is simply a pattern of light and dark which has no inherent meaning (see Figure 2.2). What I 'see' in the inkblot is an interpretation I give to the light and dark pattern. Others will interpret the light and dark pattern in different ways. There is no 'right' way to interpret the inkblot, no meaning it 'really' contains. Similarly, what each individual 'sees' in the world is an interpretation of the immense mass of data which exists. As with the inkblot, what we 'see' in the world may be influenced by numerous factors, including the current context in which it is 'seen', meaning structures we have created in the past and genetic factors. Each of us, then, constructs the world and for each of us the construction is different. In a sense learning is about giving meaning to the world. Paulo Freire (1970), the great Brazilian educator and revolutionary, referred to learning as 'naming the world', and in a real sense this is what learning is: creating order and giving meaning to the world.

Figure 2.2   An inkblot

Each of us having a unique interpretation of the world is an obvious inhibitor to communication. When we talk together about some subject such as 'leadership' your understanding may be based on such a different meaning structure from mine that it makes it hard for us to understand what each other means. It is little wonder that we must work so hard at communication. But the uniqueness born of individual interpretation has very positive and important consequences as well. It is because we each construct the world, rather than mentally copy or record it, that we are able to generate diverse new ideas and understandings. This diversity, created by each person's unique construction of the world, makes us, as a species, creative and intelligent. And further, it is this difference between these individual interpretations that stimulates further learning.

We create meaning structures both intentionally and unintentionally. Meaning structures are created intentionally when we are purposively trying to understand or learn something. I will call that 'comprehension activity'. The unintentional creation of meaning structures occurs outside of our conscious awareness: 'tacit comprehension'. Although the latter is more frequent, the former is more fully understood, so we shall address it first.

Comprehension activity takes place in a metaphorical processing space referred to as 'working memory' (sometimes misnamed 'short-term memory'). In this space, relationships are developed between parts of data that we have taken in. Meaning structures that we have developed in the past are retrieved and are related to the new meaning that is being developed. The reconstructed meaning is then stored in a metaphorical space called 'long-term memory'. Long-term memory contains all that we 'know'. But what we know is not stored in the syntax of spoken language; rather, it is stored as an expanding set of relationships, any one bit of data having relationships to many other bits of data in a weblike configuration. Meaning structures built of multiple relationships allow for a kind of flexibility that could not occur with natural language storage. And flexibility is paramount, because we alter our meaning structures each time we retrieve them to relate them to new data.

I use the term 'metaphorical' because researchers do not postulate a literal space where either working or long-term memory reside. The terms to describe this metaphorical space are borrowed from computer language, so we are using the computer, which we understand, to illustrate what happens in the human process of learning, which we understand much less well. By using the computer as an analogy, we facilitate our thinking about learning, but we also constrain it. The computer is a linear, sequential processor, while human learning is both linear and holistic. Our learning is linear, in that much is comprehended through the linear media of spoken and written language, but we are also able to grasp the subtleness of non-verbal meaning and the context in which an event is occurring in a holistic way, which the computer cannot do.

The meaning structures we develop are linked with other meaning structures to form networks. In this way everything we know is somehow related to everything else we know. The whole of one individual's network is his or her 'cognitive map'. When I use the term 'cognitive' here, I am not intending to limit the relationships to areas of formal knowledge, nor to that which is only in conscious awareness, but I include as well all the feelings, beliefs, motor skills, procedures, and a host of unnamed expressions of our understanding. We have no term to represent all of what we know. We are so used to dividing our knowing into knowledge and feelings. But by using the term cognitive map, I intend to encompass both feelings and knowledge, both tacit and explicit.

The more ways a meaning structure is tied (i.e. ways in which it is related) to our existing cognitive map the more likely we are to be able to retrieve it at a later time. It is difficult to retrieve a new meaning structure that bears little relationship to the existing cognitive map: for example, foreign words, scientific terms or directions that include unfamiliar landmarks are difficult to retrieve after a few minutes because we have few ways to connect these to what is already in our long-term memory. But that also means that the more we learn (that is the larger

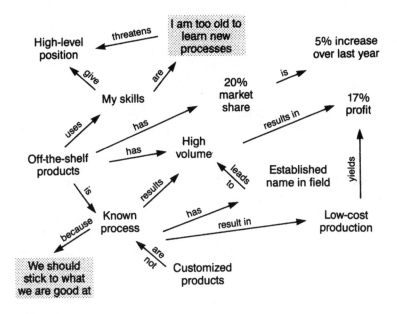

Figure 2.3　Sharon's long-term memory

our cognitive map and the more the meaning structures within it are interrelated) the more we increase our capacity to learn – the capability of tying new information to the cognitive map is increased. So rather than filling up our long-term memory over time, we are increasing its storage capability.

Figures 2.3–2.6 show a very simplistic example of the process of creating meaning structures. Figure 2.3 is a representational map of the meaning structures (relationships among data) in a small part of Sharon's total long-term memory. Sharon has developed meaning structures related to the off-the-shelf products which her company sells. In the map each data bit is related in several different ways to other bits of data. Those relationships are shown with arrows and the nature of each relation is indicated by the label on the arrow. We might summarize the interpretation Sharon has given to the data she has about off-the-shelf products as:

Our company has 20% of the off-the-shelf product market which is a 5% increase over last year. We are able to obtain this high volume, which has resulted in 17% profit, because we have developed a low-cost process. We have an established name in the field that gives us this high volume. We should stick to what we know how to do well. I have the skills needed in the off-the-shelf product business and that has resulted in my obtaining a high-level position in this organization. We should not get into the customized products business, about which we have little understanding.

In Figure 2.4 we see the same map along with some new information that Jack is providing for Sharon and others at a briefing. By the facts and figures Jack provides he appears to be advocating that the company consider developing a line of customized products given that there is a new technology that could lower production costs for customized products.

In Figure 2.5 we again see the same segment of Sharon's long-term memory, alongside the information that Jack is providing, and an illustration of how Sharon is relating data in her working memory to the new information. We see that she has taken in some, but not all, of what Jack said and is retrieving related meaning structures from her own long-term memory that are related to what Jack has said.

The final figure in this series (Figure 2.6) again shows Sharon's long-term memory, now reconstructed with some of Jack's information. Her reconstructed map includes the idea that this new technology may make customized products lower cost, but includes as well some doubts about the information because of what she knows of Jack from the past. The new information also appears to have raised some confusion for her about whether the company should stick to what it knows how to do (illustrated by the slash marks across the arrow). These figures illustrate Sharon's comprehension activity as she attempts to make sense of new data she has taken in and to relate it to the meaning structures which she already has in long-term memory.

We may construct meaning structures intentionally, as described in this example. However, we have another way of learning that is less volitional, although it still involves the

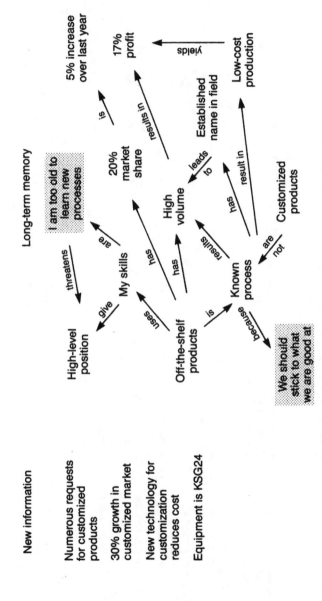

Figure 2.4 Introduction of new information into Sharon's current understanding

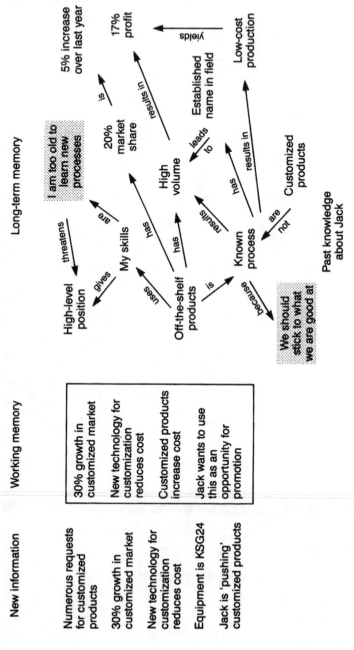

Figure 2.5   Integration of new information into Sharon's long-term memory

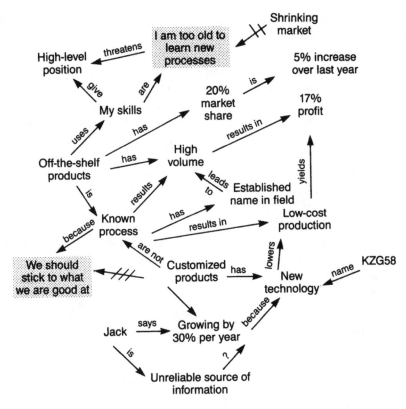

Figure 2.6   **Revised map of Sharon's long-term memory**

development of relationships and their storage in long-term memory. This second way of learning occurs over time and without conscious awareness. It is the way young children, for example, learn language, by hearing it and creating patterns in the words and syntax, yet remaining unaware of the patterns. The child is aware only that he or she is able to communicate, but not of the syntax learned to facilitate the construction of sentences.

It is not only children who learn tacitly. Much of the knowledge we as adults carry about ourselves and others is learned through tacit comprehension. Our ideas about abstractions such as beauty, justice, love and freedom have been learned tacitly from exposure to the culture in which we live. When we join a new organization as an adult employee, we learn how to act, what to say and what is expected. Much of this cultural information is learned, not by someone conveying it verbally, but from working in the organization over a period of time. A young woman, just out of law school who has recently joined a firm, may find herself 'acting like a lawyer' without ever having made a conscious decision to act differently than she did as a student. She has learned these new behaviours through tacit comprehension.

Our meaning structures take many forms including visual and auditory images, rules, concepts, beliefs about people and ourselves, attitudes and values, motor skills, inferences, and rules for thinking. Meaning structures are also constructed about feelings, such as hate, love, joy, awe and anger; beauty, as in music, art and dance; and images, such as faces, gestures and shapes. The smell of vanilla may be related to an idea, the emotion experienced upon hearing Beethoven's *Ode to Joy* may be related to a person or an event and the sight of the Lincoln Memorial may be related to our sense of freedom or justice. All that we know we know, and all that we do not know we know, but do know, is stored as meaning structures.

I have used the word 'stored', but the image of putting an object into storage, which is later retrieved looking much the same as when we put it in, would be an inaccurate picture of how we store and retrieve meaning. Meaning that is retrieved from long-term memory is always reconstructed. We alter the relationships between parts in the retrieval process. An analogy might be rather than retrieving your bicycle from the garage you select from a whole garage full of parts and build up the bicycle each time you retrieve it. The general shape of the bicycle might be consistent, but the particular wing nuts, seat or frame colour might differ each time. Thus, we construct our remembrances. No wonder they vary so greatly in the telling.

Learning and truth

The representational map of Sharon's long-term memory (Figure 2.6) shows that the name she has related to the new technology is KZG58. The name Jack reported at the briefing was KSG24. We can say that this particular relationship stored in Sharon's long-term memory is wrong. And although it is a small inaccuracy, one which she can correct the next time she is exposed to information related to the equipment, it nevertheless illustrates that the meaning structures we build may not be accurate. At another level we could say that perhaps KZG58 would be a more fitting name for the equipment, or even that Sharon knows something about the equipment of which Jack is ignorant. But if, for the moment, we take at face value that Sharon has misremembered the name of the equipment, we can say that the meaning structure she has built is inaccurate.

Individuals have a number of human limitations that result in them developing and holding meaning structures which may not be accurate. These include a tendency to look for evidence that supports their initial view rather than seeking disconfirming evidence, to generalize from small samples or single instances (Feld, 1986), and to give greater weight to more recent events. Humans are inclined to perceive the world through the lens of past events, to create self-fulfilling prophecies, and to fail to check out the inferences they make from incomplete data (March et al., 1991).

Even taking into consideration these troublesome human fallacies, the ability that humans have to create relationships and patterns is extraordinary. There are virtually no limits to our understanding – there are always new relationships to build, new ways to 'see' the world. We can, in fact, invent the world with this wonderful ability. We can, as Robert Kennedy said, 'see things that never were'. If our minds were *only* able to record the external world accurately, we would not be able to create such splendid new worlds. If the price of imagination is the human propensity for error, perhaps it is cheap at the cost!

We are, however, still left with the difficult problem of how we can know if the meaning structures we develop are true. Bateson (1979) cautions:

> Let us say that truth would mean a precise correspondence between our description and what we describe or between our total network of abstractions and deductions and some total understanding of the outside world. Truth in this sense is not obtainable. And even if we ignore the barriers of coding, the circumstance that our description will be in words or figures or pictures but that what we describe is going to be in flesh and blood and action – even disregarding that hurdle of translation, we shall never be able to claim final knowledge of anything whatsoever. (p. 27)

He concludes that we cannot know if our meaning structures are true. Yet, in order to function in the world we must act 'as if' the meaning structures that we have constructed are true. And at the same time we must strive to remember that there are other relationships that we do not see – so that we are ever open to another way of seeing the world. It is all too easy to forget that we have created the world in which we live.

Development of meaning structures

The new meaning the individual constructs may confirm or alter the existing meaning structures that the individual has in long-term memory. Much of the data we take in confirms the meaning that we have already constructed. In part this happens because existing meaning structures influence both what the individual attends to or ignores and how data are interpreted. Individuals appear to have a preference for interpreting the world in terms of their existing meaning structures, which is another way of saying we often see what we expect to see. If the individual has developed a meaning structure about Mary, a co-worker, that 'Mary is shy', the individual may interpret many of Mary's actions, both verbal and non-verbal, as examples of her shyness. Another co-worker who has developed a different meaning structure about Mary, for example, 'Mary is aloof' might interpret those same actions as examples of aloofness. Moreover, individuals appear to attend more to information that supports their existing meaning structure than to information that might refute it.

When we notice information that conflicts with our existing meaning structure, we experience an internal sense of discomfort or dissonance. Human beings appear to be strongly motivated to reduce the dissonance created by information that conflicts with existing meaning structures. For example, one of the effective and intentional uses of dissonance in management development programmes is to provide participants with feedback about how others view them, which, if discrepant with how the individuals see their own behaviour, motivates them to change. To reduce the dissonance we experience we can either deny the validity of the new information ('What do they know anyway?') or process the new information comparing it with the existing meaning structures until a new understanding is reached, that is, reconstruct the meaning structures. 'Dissonance' is another way of saying 'difference'. So we are back to the importance of difference to learning.

Relationship of meaning structures to action

Our actions are mediated by our meaning structures. Action, as the term is used here, includes words as well as a physical response, and even includes instructions to others to carry out some course of action. It is possible for us to construct or reconstruct meaning structures without them resulting in noticeable action. The opposite, however, is not possible; in order for us to take any new action our meaning structures must change in some way. Figure 2.7 illustrates a meaning structure that a member of an organization, Jane, has developed out of her

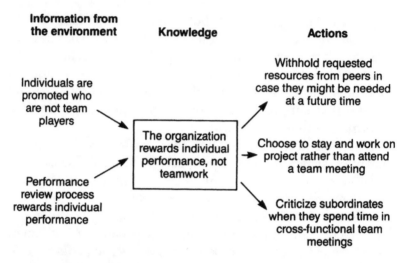

Figure 2.7   Relationship between knowledge and action

experience in that organization over time: 'The organization rewards individual performance, not teamwork'. We can say that this is what Jane believes or knows or has come to understand. The arrows to the right of this statement illustrate how this meaning structure might mediate certain actions. The first action suggests that holding this meaning might result in Jane refraining from sharing resources with her team members, the second that she might skip some team meetings if they interfere with her own individual performance, and the third that she might put pressure on her subordinates not to spend too much time in cross-functional team meetings. The left-hand column suggests some of the experiences that Jane has had that have led her to construct the meaning structure. She has interpreted these experiences to derive the meaning 'The organization rewards individual performance not teamwork'.

If the organization hopes to change Jane's actions, displayed on the right, Jane will first have to change the meaning structure that is driving her actions. We would not expect, nor want, her to act in ways that did not make sense to her. To change her meaning structure Jane will have to have some new experiences (reflected on the left) that she can interpret in a different way, or perhaps she can reframe that experience as 'past' and, based on the promise of the organization, define the present as different. In any case, it is the meaning she makes that will mediate her actions.

It is of course possible that Jane has other meaning structures, also learned in the context of the organization, that imply that it would be wise to give lip service to teamwork even if she believes the organization does not truly value it. It is such conflicting meaning structures derived from both the mixed messages of the organization and from the undiscussability of such messages that make organizational change so difficult.

Meaning structures, then, mediate action. It is, however, not possible to determine an individual's meaning structures from their actions. Any one action may be mediated by a host of different meaning structures. Jane may attend the team meetings because she values the team, thinks it is expected of her, is trying to get better acquainted with a co-worker, or a host of other reasons. We cannot know what meaning structures an individual has from observing his or her behaviour.

Limitations of working memory

As human beings we have a limited amount of processing space, and that consideration influences much about the way we learn. Our processing space in working memory appears to be limited to seven (plus or minus two) unrelated bits of data (Miller, 1956). Much more than seven bits and we begin to lose some of the data we are trying to hold on to. Seven digit telephone numbers are about at our limit. It helps to conserve space in working memory if we can put several bits together as one 'chunk', for example, the first three digits of a telephone number chunk as a recognizable section of the community, or five different ways to analyse data we can chunk as 'statistical tools'. When items are chunked we no longer have to hold the individual items but can hold the 'chunk' in our processing space. When we need to we can disaggregate the chunk back into its parts.

The importance of 'chunking', which is another way of saying 'categorizing' data, is that we can then relate larger chunks of data to each other. We are able to build new relationships only among the data which we are able to hold in working memory simultaneously – within our limited processing space. So, the better our ability to chunk data (organize it into categories) the greater the level of complexity with which we can think. Complexity is another way of saying that the individual can find relationships among larger chunks.

Often we find that the more familiar we are with a 'field' of study, the easier it is for us to find categories within it and to find ways those larger categories relate to each other. An example comes from research with chess experts. Surprisingly there is no strategy difference between chess masters and less expert players. Gagné and Glaser (1987) provide this comparison of expert and novice chess players:

All looked ahead about the same number of moves as they tried to evaluate each move, and used the same strategy to guide this search. However, experts simply recognized the best move and gave it first consideration, evaluating the other moves only as a way of double-checking themselves. When experts look at an apparently complicated situation, they are able to represent it in terms of a small number of patterns or chunks. This ability to perceive the problem in a way that restricts the problem space has since been shown to occur in other areas as well. (p. 69)

A second way in which limited processing space influences our learning is that it necessitates making many of our meaning structures *tacit* so that we do not have to deal with them in our conscious awareness. Those meaning structures that we use repeatedly are candidates for becoming tacit, particularly those that do not change much over time. Familiar examples would include motor skills, such as the commands of a word processor or how to work the tricky lock on our door; frequently used interpersonal skills, such as how to respond to a greeting, or react to someone's anger; self-perception, such as how we think about ourselves as smart or kind; and beliefs we hold, such as justice, what is worth striving for, and what is right. To hold such meaning structures tacitly does not mean they are forgotten; rather, they are temporarily lost to conscious awareness.

Actions that are based on tacit meaning structures are *automatic*. They do not need to be thought about, that is they do not need to pass through working memory to be reconstructed and then used. Bateson (1979) says that:

No organism can afford to be conscious of matters with which it could deal at an unconscious level. Broadly we can afford to sink those sorts of knowledge which continue to be true regardless of changes in the environment, but we maintain in an accessible place all those controls of behaviour which must be modified for every instance. The lion can sink into his unconscious the propositions that zebras are his natural prey, but in dealing with any particular zebra he must be able to modify the movements of his attack to fit with the particular terrain and the particular evasive tactics of the particular zebra. (pp. 142–3)

We are often unaware that we have a particular tacit meaning structure until that meaning is challenged. An example of a tacit meaning structure that many organizational members in the US have held is the appropriateness of upper-level management being paid salaries that are up to 100 times greater than first-line employees in the same organization. Recently this assumption has been challenged in the media, and thus has come into the conscious awareness of many organizational employees, who have begun to question whether such a differential is appropriate.

A great deal of the interaction that human beings have with each other is informed by tacit meaning structures. Interaction is simply too swift for individuals to take the time to process every aspect of it. Thus, how an individual responds to praise, to disappointment, to confusion, to embarrassment, etc. involves tacit meaning structures. For example, when I want to tell another person that he or she is acting inappropriately, I might make a joke of my criticism. Embedding the criticism in a joke is not a plan that I think through on the spot (as in, 'This person will react less defensively if I make a joke of this than if I am serious'); rather, it is a meaning structure I have developed for dealing with uncomfortable situations and have used frequently enough that it has become tacit and can therefore happen automatically. My exact choice of words may be processed on the spot, but the process of how to tell another person about their inappropriate behaviour may be tacit. Some theorists have suggested that as much as 90 per cent of human meaning structures are tacit.

The benefits of making meaning structures tacit are the freeing up of processing space and the ability to respond more quickly than conscious processing allows. There are, however, serious limitations that tacit meaning structures impose upon our learning as well. One limitation is the difficulty in testing the validity of tacit meaning structures. A second limitation, not unrelated to the first, is the difficulty of changing tacit meaning structures. A third limitation is the propensity to construct and employ untested inferences.

Explicit meaning structures, those that remain in conscious awareness, are put to a kind of test each time we engage in comprehension activity related to them. If a meaning structure we retrieve from long-term memory does not fit new data, and the new data are convincing, we will most likely change the meaning structure before returning it to long-term memory. Functioning in the world provides us with an ongoing check of the explicit meaning we have created for ourselves.

Tacit meaning structures do not, however, receive that continual correction process. We employ tacit structures without recalling them to working memory and without the active comparison to new data. The result is that it is possible to continue employing tacit meaning structures that perhaps worked well for us in the past, but due to changing circumstances no longer do. For example, before the emphasis on quality it was a commonly held axiom that improving quality increased costs. Before the 1980s most organizational members would not have thought about testing that meaning structure.

It is even possible to hold tacit meaning structures that contradict explicit meaning structures. For example, a manager may hold the *tacit* belief that workers need clear and precise directions and the *explicit* belief that workers act more productively if involved in selecting their own goals – and be unaware of the contradiction in the two beliefs. When conflicting meaning structures exist an individual is likely to act in ways that others see as inconsistent. In the above example, employees may interpret the manager's inconsistency as an intent to deceive, when, in fact, the manager may be unaware of the contradiction because of the tacit nature of one of the meaning structures.

Argyris and Schon (1978) go further, to say that not only might we be unaware of the inconsistency between our explicit and tacit meaning structures (they would use the terms 'espoused theories' and 'theories in use') but that we actually design processes to keep us blind to the discrepancies – and that these designed processes are also tacit. To return to an earlier example in which I used a joke to give negative information to someone. I postulated that the meaning structure which provides the 'joke strategy' is tacit, although the specific language that corresponds with the situation is not. The recipient of the 'joke' is required by norms of politeness to laugh – an implied acknowledgement of the truth of the negative inference of the joke. If the recipient were to take the 'joke' seriously by trying to correct the misperception he or she would be considered a poor sport: after all 'it was only a joke'. The recipient is placed in a position in which the inaccuracy cannot be corrected without the individual appearing to be a poor sport. I, as the joke teller, have effectively designed a process in which it is unlikely that I will receive information that corrects the negative perception I have. And even this process, the process that keeps me blind to my own error, is tacit.

In order to alter tacit meaning structures, it is first necessary to become aware of them – a major problem, since it is difficult to become aware of that of which you are unaware. Perspective appears necessary if individuals are to become aware of that which is tacit. Our tacit meaning structures are like a frame in which we are embedded, and perspective allows us to view ourselves and our actions from outside the frame. Others, who are significantly different from us, can often provide that perspective for us. Working in another country, visiting an organization that is using a process we thought impossible, or sometimes even outdoor adventure programmes, are other ways to gain perspective on our current frame.

To alter a tacit meaning structure we must first become aware of it, and must then be able to recognize the dissonance between it and the new information. We must actively alter the meaning structure and, if it is related to actions that happen rapidly, must practise to make the actions automatic again. It may, in fact, take a lengthy period of time before responses become automatic enough to be useful again in most situations. Anyone who has attempted to use the commands of a new word processing program, or to employ new communication skills, recognizes in themselves a lack of spontaneity. Until new meaning structures are automatic, interaction responses may, in fact, appear to others to be 'false' or 'put on'.

Finally, the ability humans have to draw inferences from sparse data is both a great advantage and a considerable problem. To infer means to draw a conclusion. We make hundreds of necessary inferences each day. We predict how people will act from past behaviour; we infer that a problem exists in the accounting department because the statements are late; we infer that there is discrimination because we did not get promoted. Without the ability to draw inferences we would be limited to trial and error learning, never able to make the leaps in thought that can save us time and energy and allow us to deal with significant complexity. The difficulty with inferences comes not because we make them, but because we are inclined to regard our inferences as fact rather than hypothesis. Holding them as fact, we see no need to test them.

Inferences are retained as meaning structures in long-term memory while the original data on which the inference was based are often forgotten. The meaning structure influences the individual's interpretation of future actions and events, thus creating self-fulfilling prophecies. For example, individuals who infer discrimination because they were passed over for promotion are likely to interpret future slights as discrimination and as a result may begin to act in a hostile manner toward those whom they believe are being discriminatory. If the original inference was incorrect, such individuals have now developed a situation in which they are unlikely to discover that. It is also possible that the original inference was correct and discrimination is occurring; because it is an inference does not mean it is incorrect, only that it is untested.

The solution that Argyris and Schon (1978) propose is not to refrain from making inferences, but rather to test our inferences immediately. We typically fail to do that for four reasons:

1   We consider our inferences as fact and therefore see no need to test them.
2   We are embarrassed to talk about the inference, particularly if we hold a negative inference that could turn out to be wrong.
3   We presume that others would be less than truthful about acknowledging the accuracy of our inference or at least be very defensive if it is correct.
4   We cannot see a non-threatening way to test the inference.

Meta-cognition

A type of meaning structure that is of particular importance to the improvement of learning is meta-cognition: our knowledge of our own cognitive processes. Meta-cognition refers to the active monitoring of learning processes, such as self-questioning (Do I now understand this or do I need to read it again?); persistence (how long we will keep trying to make sense of confusing data); relating data sets (asking myself how a piece of equipment (or theory) differs from or is the same as another); purposefully seeking new information (What do I need to learn in order to understand this situation?); and questioning inferences (What data am I basing this inference on and are they adequate?). Meta-cognition functions like an executive controller for our learning. Meta-cognition constitutes our learning style as well as our learning capability. Studies have shown that one thing that differentiates good and poor learners in a school setting is their meta-cognitive skills. Like other parts of our cognitive map, meta-cognition is most often tacit and therefore unavailable for testing.

The human need to learn

As human beings we appear to have a drive to learn that is, in part, a survival mechanism: we function more effectively in a world of which we have made sense (Hatano and Inagaki, 1987). We also derive pleasure from learning; there is a feeling of dissonance associated with confusion (non-understanding) which is relieved in a pleasurable way when we make meaning of ambiguous information.

Learning, however, appears to be about more than survival: it is also about human *development*, the growth of the individual. Maslow (1954) proposes that humans have a drive toward self-actualization, Rogers (1961) talks about basic actualizing tendency, and Kegan (1982) describes the evolving self. Each of these theorists, and many others, characterize development as a progression of 'frames' or lenses through which we interpret our experience. We 'learn' within the context of that frame, altering meaning structures as new information conflicts with current meaning structures. But learning also pushes against the frame, because some of what we experience cannot be understood within the existing frame and remains a nagging dissonance that is difficult to dismiss and impossible to incorporate. At some juncture the frame breaks down – there are too many discrepancies, too much the current frame cannot take into account. A major reorganization of meaning occurs which moves us from one developmental state to the next.

Each stage or period of stability is a way of seeing ourselves in relation to the external world or in the terms we have been using here, a way to organize our understanding of the world and our relationship to it. But as Kegan (1982) has pointed out it is a tenuous and temporary organization structure that we build: 'The relationship gets better organized by increasing differentiations of the self from the environment and thus by increasing integrations of the environment' (p. 113).

Kegan (1982) sees the central theme of this relationship as two basic, but conflicting yearnings of humans, one for communion (the yearning to be included, to be part of, to be close to) and one for agency (the yearning to be autonomous, to be distinct, to choose one's own direction). At various stages we find a satisfactory balance to these two yearnings, favouring one or the other. But over time the balance no longer seems satisfactory and we suffer a period of confusion out of which a new balance is constructed. This conflict between communion and agency is a central construct in many developmental theories, including those of Piaget, Kohlberg, Loevinger, Maslow, Erikson and McClelland.

Learning is central both to bringing about the massive reorganization that causes us to have a new sense of self in relation to the world, and to constructing a satisfactory existence within our current frame.

This need to learn serves many important ends for us as human beings, including survival, both as individuals and as a species, career advancement, prestige, etc. But this need is also simply fundamental to who we are as human beings – we are a learning species. And although there are a considerable number of individuals who suffered so many negative experiences in formal school settings that they no longer think of themselves as learners, they are learners nonetheless.

Summary

There is a long history of theorists who have explored the relationship between experience and learning. John Dewey, Kurt Lewin and Jean Piaget are certainly seminal thinkers and have influenced the ideas of most theorists that have come after them.

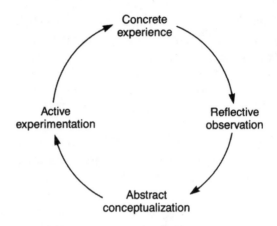

Figure 2.8   Kolb's experiential learning cycle

They inspired the work of later theorists Gregory Bateson, Reg Revans, Paulo Freire, Chris Argyris, David Kolb, Malcolm Knowles, Jack Mezirow and Alan Mumford. I have found Kolb's (1984) model of experiential learning a useful way to summarize the ideas of these theorists and thus helpful in summarizing the process of individual learning outlined in this chapter.

Kolb proposes a cycle through which individual learning progresses (see Figure 2.8). The cycle begins when we each experience the world through our senses. Kolb calls this step 'concrete experience', to indicate that he does not mean the vicarious experience we have through books or plays, but a real world experience. Examples of concrete experience could be as varied as sitting through a boring meeting or suffering the distress of losing a job. Kolb suggests that to learn from our experience we must engage in a second step of consciously reflecting on what has occurred. This step he calls 'reflective observation'. We are able to reflect on much less than what occurred in the actual experience. Reflection is selective, and as we saw earlier, is influenced by our expectations and our existing meaning. The third step in the learning cycle is making sense of what we have experienced. In the language of this book that involves relating the new information to existing meaning structures and out of that relationship creating new meaning. Kolb calls this step 'abstract conceptualization'. The final step in Kolb's model is active experimentation. At this step we test out the meaning that we have constructed by taking action in the world – which then leads to new experience. Kolb has shown that over time we tend to get more proficient at some steps of this process than at others, and thus we develop a learning style preference. But, as he has noted, all the steps are necessary, and to the extent that we slight any of the steps, our learning is less effective and complete.

Kolb defines individual learning as 'the process whereby knowledge is created through the transformation of experience'. Although the experiential learning cycle leaves out much of the detail of the learning process that I have described in this chapter, both his definition and the experiential learning cycle capture the essence, which is that:

- Learning is about interpreting what we experience in the world.
- We each create our own unique interpretation.
- The meaning we create mediates our actions.

Individual learning in the social context

In this section I have confined my discussion to how individuals learn, with the intent of using that framework to better understand how a collective might learn. But even in this discussion I have not been able to talk about individuals as isolated entities devoid of contact with others. As the sociologist George Herbert Mead (1934) said, 'Mind can never find expression, and can never come into existence at all, except in terms of a social environment' (p. 223). Individual learning is dependent upon the collective. As we turn now to collective learning we shall see that the converse is also true: collective learning is dependent upon the individual.

References

Argyris, C. and Schon, D. A. (1978). *Organizational Learning: A Theory of Action Perspective*. Reading MA: Addison-Wesley.

Bateson, G. (1979). *Mind and Nature a Necessary Unity*. New York: Ballantine.

Feld, J. (1986). 'On the difficulty of learning from experience', in Sims, H. P. et al. (eds), *The Thinking Organization*, pp. 263–92. San Francisco: Jossey-Bass.

Freire, P. (1970). *Pedagogy of the Oppressed*. Harmondsworth: Penguin.

Gagné R. M. and Glaser, R. (1987). 'Foundations in learning research', in Gagné, R. M. (ed.), *Instructional Technology: Foundations*, pp. 49–83. Hillsdale NJ: Lawrence Erlbaum Associates.

Hatano, G. and Inagaki, K. (1987). 'A theory of motivation for comprehension and its application to mathematics instruction', in Romberg, T. A. and Stewart, D. M. (eds), *The Monitoring of School Mathematics*, Background papers, Vol. 2: Implications from psychology; outcomes of instruction. Program Report 87–2, pp. 27–46. Madison WI: Center for Education Research.

Kegan, R. (1982). *The Evolving Self*. Cambridge MA: Harvard University Press.

Kolb, D. A. (1984). *Experiential Learning*. Englewood Cliffs NJ: Prentice-Hall.

March, J. G., Sproull, L. S. and Tamuz, M. (1991). 'Learning from samples of one or fewer'. *Organization Science*, **2** (1), 1–13.

Maslow, A. H. (1954). *Motivation and Personality*. New York: Harper & Row.

McCall, M. W., Lombardo, M. M. and Morrison, A. M. (1988). *The Lessons of Experience*. Lexington MA: Lexington Books.

Mead, G. H. (1934). *Mind, Self, and Society*. Chicago: University of Chicago Press.

Miller, G. A. (1956). 'The magical number seven, plus or minus two; Some limits on our capacity for processing information'. *Psychological Review*, **63**, 81–97.

Perry, W. G., Jr. (1970). *Forms of Intellectual and Ethical Development in the College Years*. New York: Holt, Rinehart & Winston.

Rogers, C. R. (1961). *On Becoming a Person: A Therapist's View of Psychotherapy*. Boston: Houghton Mifflin.

3 The hallways of learning*

Organizations are collections of individuals, each of whom has developed and stored meaning structures, is capable of creating new meaning from interfacing with the environment and each other, can test that meaning against their current meaning structures, and can alter or reconstruct their meaning structures – in other words, each organizational member can learn. An organization learns through this capability of its members. Organizational learning is not simply the sum of all that its organizational members know, rather it is the collective use of this capability of learning. It is a verb, not a noun. Argyris and Schon (1978) explain: ' . . . there is no organizational learning without individual learning, and that individual learning is a necessary but insufficient condition for organizational learning' (p. 20). To understand how organizational learning differs from individual learning it is helpful to think of organizational

* This chapter is adapted from an article first published in *Organizational Dynamics*, Spring, 1997. My Thanks to Tom Carter, former vice-president of HR at Alcoa, for the term 'hallways'.

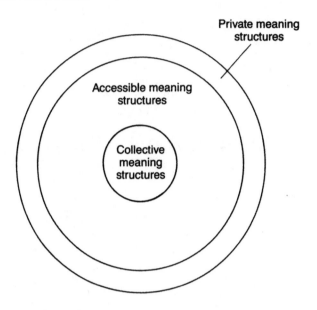

Figure 3.1   Three types of meaning structure

members as having meaning structures that could be categorized as private, accessible and collective (McClellan, 1983).

Private meaning

Each and every individual in an organization constructs meaning for themselves. They make sense of what is happening – in their organization, with their co-workers, with their customers; they attend classes, read books, talk with experts; they plan, strategize and reflect. They engage in a continual process of constructing meaning and of reconstructing it yet again, as they encounter new experiences and ideas. Over time, individuals, using this most basic of human processes, accumulate a great deal of knowledge and expertise about their organization and about their job. We could envision a whole organization full of individuals who each possess extensive knowledge and expertise – and yet the *organization* may not be learning because these individuals keep private the meaning that they construct; they keep their meaning making within the walls of their private office. We could liken private meaning to a private office, a place where meaning is protected and others do not have access to it.

Private meaning, then, is that meaning which the individual constructs but does not make accessible to others in the organization. For example, imagine a field representative who installs and repairs the company's product, and over time determines that a certain part fails repeatedly under certain identifiable conditions. This is private meaning the field representative has constructed. Unless the field representative talks with others about the meaning he or she is developing, the organization will not learn.

There can, of course, be very legitimate reasons for individuals keeping the meaning they construct to themselves, for example:

- the meaning may be about personal issues that are of little value to the organization
- the meaning may have been constructed from information that would violate someone's confidence to reveal.

There may also be political or logistical reasons for holding meaning private, for example:

- an individual may see a competitive advantage to her or himself by keeping the meaning quiet
- an individual may have tried in the past to convey information and concluded that others are not interested in his or her ideas
- there may be no easily accessible channel through which the meaning can be conveyed.

Though there are understandable reasons for keeping meaning private, the more that individuals are willing to make the meaning they are constructing available to others in the organization, the more the organization is able to learn.

Figure 3.2   Organizational meaning structures

Accessible meaning

A second category of meaning is that which individuals *do* make available to others in the organization – it is analogous to the hallways of the organization where important exchanges take place. This analogy is attractive because we recognize hallways as places where some of our best conversations have occurred. Ask any conference attendee and you are likely to hear the familiar comment, 'The sessions were okay, but I had some *great* hallway conversations'. Hallways, whether at a conference or at work, have a very different feel from most meeting rooms and offices. There is less sense of hierarchy in hallways where everyone seems a more equal participant. Hallway conversations often involve multiple perspectives because anyone who wanders by can join in, adding their ideas to the mix. By the same token, people feel free to walk away if the subject proves uninteresting because the organizational norms that require we feign interest in a topic, are not applicable in our hallways. We talk more freely and openly in the hallway – perhaps we also talk in more depth, being more willing to raise those subjects that are of concern to us but that seem undiscussable in other settings.

Hallways are places where ideas get tested against the thinking of others. As long as meaning is held privately it is protected from the discovery that it may be wrong or limited in perspective. When it is made accessible to others then the data on which it is based can be challenged and the reasoning and logic that led to conclusions can be examined.

Hallways are places where *collective meaning* is made – in other words, meaning is not just exchanged, it is *constructed* in the dialogue between organizational members. In the process of each person articulating his or her own meaning and of comprehending how it differs from that which others have constructed, individuals alter the meaning they hold. The act of articulating the meaning each has constructed serves to clarify it for the speaker as well as the listener. Individuals often do not know what meaning they have made until they attempt to put it into words. The meaning each organizational member articulates influences others. Influence does not necessarily imply agreement, but it does suggest a cognizance or recognition. Out of this confluence of ideas, new meaning develops, meaning that no one individual brought into the hallway. It is this joint construction of meaning that is organizational learning.

It would be inaccurate to equate hallways with the dissemination of organizational information, although a full and complete exchange of organizational data is absolutely necessary for the hallways to lead to organizational learning. But, data have little meaning in and of themselves. Organizational members imbue the numbers and figures they see with meaning – and the meaning that is imbued legitimately differs from member to member. When organizational members read that the turnover rate is 25 per cent, calculate that the product development cycle is eighteen months long, or hear that the organization failed to get the anticipated 3 million dollar contract, each assigns different meaning to the data, not just in terms of cause but also of importance, of possibilities, etc.

As Bolman and Deal (1991) have suggested, what is most important about any event is *not* what happened, but *what it means* and, because events and meanings are loosely coupled, the same event can have very different meanings to different people. Organizational members always construct their own meaning for the data and events of the organization. To the extent that meaning is made privately, it remains unique to each individual; to the extent that it is constructed jointly, the organization learns.

The categorical boundary between private and accessible meaning is gradual and flexible. For example, individuals may be willing to make their meaning accessible under some circumstances but not under others, or they may be willing to communicate their meaning only to select members of the organization. Thus the same meaning may sometimes be private and sometimes accessible.

Collective meaning

Collective meaning is that which organizational members hold in common. These are the norms, strategies and assumptions which specify how work gets done and what work is important to do. Collective meaning may be codified in policies and procedures, but to be collective it must also reside in the minds of organizational members. Organizational members create the collective meaning, yet it can become so familiar that they forget they created it and begin to think it is simply the 'way things are'. For example, it may be tacitly understood that whatever else happens you do not miss your schedule, that top management will be selected from individuals within the finance group, or that people cover for each other to take care of family responsibilities.

Collective meaning is like having a *storeroom* where the mementos of the past are kept. It is extremely important to an organization – it is its history. Collective meaning is the glue that holds organizational members together and allows them to act in concert with each other. It provides a sense of belonging and community. It saves the organization time – there is no need for lengthy discussions about those issues that organizational members are all in agreement about – that can be spent on more critical issues.

Collective meaning can, however, have a negative impact on the organization. In a rapidly changing world, collective meaning that was advantageous at one point in time may have become obsolete. If this meaning is tacit, it may be unavailable to the organization for examination. Thus, an organization can maintain collective meaning that is dysfunctional without real-izing it. There are many organizational examples that are apparent in hindsight, for example, IBM's view of the future of personal computers, or GM's ideas about what the American public wanted in their cars.

Collective meaning makes the introduction of new ideas that conflict with the existing meaning very difficult to implement. Collective meaning is viewed, by those who hold it, as 'truth'. It is not questioned because members have no need to question what they know from long years of experience to be so. For example, when Deming introduced quality concepts into the US, many organizations knew from experience that improving quality could only be achieved by greatly increased cost. That meaning was so well accepted that many organizations could not even entertain the alternative, that quality could actually reduce costs. It is only in retrospect that we can see how limiting that collective meaning was to US industry.

Although the collective meaning of an organization does change gradually and over time, as witnessed by the change in the meaning now more generally held about the relationship between quality and cost, it is difficult to change collective meaning radically or suddenly because organizational members continually reaffirm their collective meaning with each other. By definition, collective meaning is that meaning which all members hold in common. Therefore, interaction between organizational members related to collective meaning will lack differences in perspective. When everyone is in agreement there is no one to challenge the accepted position.

That collective meaning is difficult to change does not imply that it is static. It is in fact, continually being reconstructed and reaffirmed, continually being made. Although the image of a storeroom would suggest a place where items remain unchanged, in our analogous organizational storeroom meaning is constantly being recreated in the same way a ritual continually reaffirms the meaning associated with it.

Organizations learn in the hallways

Hallways are the only space in which it is possible for an organization to learn. It cannot learn in the private offices, although individual learning can certainly take place there. It cannot learn in the storeroom – although the collective meaning is continually reinforced there, *new meaning* cannot be constructed in the storeroom. If organizations are going to learn they will need to construct hallways in which the learning can occur. The real hallways of our organizations will not suffice for the level of organizational learning that is necessary. Organizations need to develop processes which have the positive characteristics of real hallways, yet are more focused and intentional. Hallways, as the term is used here, are intentional systemwide processes organizations employ to facilitate the construction of collective meaning. There are a wide variety of processes that can serve this function. Dialogue groups, network meetings, town halls; 'whole system in the room' processes such as WorkOut (GE), Strategic Search Conferences (Weisbord, 1992), Real Time Strategic Change (Jacobs, 1994), Open Space Technology (Owen, 1991), the Conference Model (Emery, 1993), and Team Syntegrity (Beer, 1994); action learning groups (Revans, 1983), scenario planning processes (Schwartz, 1991), Learning Maps (Root Learning), and Appreciative Inquiry (Cooperrider, 1995). Some of these are described in detail in

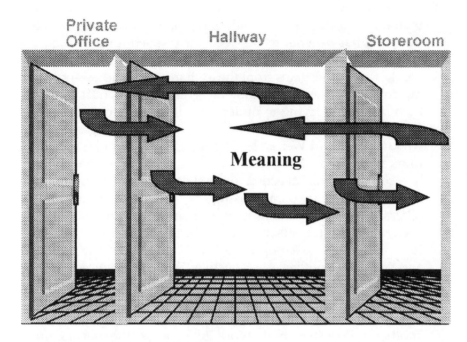

Figure 3.3 Development of hallways

Chapter 6. One of the very encouraging signs in organizations is the number and variety of hallways being developed. They are a testament to the growing interest in collective learning and to the ability of organizations to develop new organizational processes.

As varied as the current processes are, it is possible to derive common characteristics that may represent the critical elements that any such process would need in order to facilitate collective meaning. There are six such elements.

1 Dialogue not speeches

Hallways require organizational members to interact with each other, exchanging their data, conclusions, reasoning and questions with others, rather than listening to speeches or presentations. Although learning by *talking* rather than listening goes against conventional wisdom, recent studies have shown that the act of orally summarizing information works to strengthen the speaker's understanding of that information. Although the potential benefits to the receiver of such an exchange are apparent, there is evidence that it is the speaker who makes the greatest cognitive gains from the exchange. Individuals organize information differently if they are going to present it to others than if they are trying to understand it for their own sake. It is in the act of speaking that we tend to cognitively organize what we know. As Karl Weick (1995) puts it, 'How can I know what I think until I see what I say?' (p. 61).

A second beneficial action to the speaker is perspective taking, that is, the act of paraphrasing the ideas and arguments of others. Perspective taking is more than just being able to play back others' arguments in order to check with them for accuracy. It is the ability to comprehend and voice how the situation appears from another's perspective. When one voices the perspective of another, that action inclines the other to disclose information more fully than if the perspective was not voiced. The additional information and the fuller comprehension of another perspective both work to increase the development of new knowledge out of varying perspectives on a complex issue. It is necessary, however, to hold both one's own and others' perspectives in mind simultaneously to create new knowledge. Simply listening to another's perspective is less facilitative of the creation of new knowledge than giving voice to the other's perspective.

Collective learning occurs in hallways, then, because this metaphorical time and space is designed to facilitate in-depth conversation between organizational members about subjects that matter to them.

2   Egalitarian

Collective learning is more effective when organizational members talk with each other as equals rather than as disparate members of a hierarchy. Unfortunately, the culture of many organizations is such that it is difficult for those in positions of lesser authority to openly challenge the ideas of those in higher authority or even to offer alternative perspectives. Without the free flow of ideas, learning is severely limited.

Hierarchy can be a great inhibitor of collective learning. Hallways are designed as places where managers leave their positions at the door and where ideas are judged on their worth, not on who put them forth. The role of upper-level management in the hallway is often limited to that of participant, with no management speeches (whether intended to set the stage or praise the good work accomplished), that sets management apart or highlights the structural differences between people. The gathering is facilitated, when that is necessary, by non-management professionals.

3 Multiple perspectives

Difference fosters collective learning. We learn only when there is a discrepancy between how we are currently thinking about something and some event or data that calls our current thinking into question. To the extent that we all agree, or that we detect no difference, we will not learn. Thus there is a need to invite multiple perspectives into the hallway and moreover to tolerate the tension that results from the ensuing differences long enough that new meaning can be generated from them. Analogous to the need for an individual to simultaneously hold two perspectives in his or her mind in order to generate new meaning, the collective must also simultaneously *contain* multiple meanings. The longer the tension is tolerated the more possible fresh ideas will emerge. Thus hallways intentionally invite in multiple perspectives, actively encourage those perspectives to challenge accepted practice, and steadfastly maintain the ensuing tension while new learning emerges.

It is helpful to consider Weick's (1995) differentiation of ambiguous data from lack of data or ignorance. As he notes, there is a tendency to treat many organizational problems as lack of data, the hoped for solution being found in additional information. However, most organizational problems do not require more information for resolution, rather it is the problem itself that needs to be reframed – to ask different questions instead of gathering more information about the same questions. When hallways encourage multiple perspectives, the likelihood that someone will offer a useful way to reframe the problems the organization faces, increases substantially.

One of the most advantageous outcomes of fostering multiple perspectives is the opportunity it affords the collective to become aware of the tacit assumptions that are held as a group and of which they are unaware. Once noticed, tacit assumptions can be publicly discussed and their accuracy and usefulness debated. Those assumptions that have become outdated or handicapping to the organization can be discarded and those that still serve the common interest can be maintained. Without initial awareness, however, neither can happen and organizational members remain blinded by their own unawareness.

4   Non-expert based

Two fundamental assumptions that underlie hallways are:

- ordinary people, thinking together, have the capability to generate workable answers to the problems of the organization, and
- there is not just one solution to most organizational problems – there are many potential solutions, which, if agreed upon would be effective.

In the natural world the task of science is taken to be to 'discover' those laws that are 'true' and thus can predict the behaviour of natural forces. Because the natural sciences have been so beneficial and are so admired, it is tempting to assume that it is possible to 'discover' answers in human systems that would also allow the accurate prediction of outcomes. To this end, organizations often seek experts who can provide the hoped for *answer* – the search involves the latest management books, well-known consultants and highly paid speakers. But the world of human systems is *constructed* out of *meaning* – organizations, including churches, schools, nations and families, are products of how those involved think about them – and, as we are well aware, different cultures think about them differently. Thus in human systems, meaning is 'constructed' rather than 'discovered'. Expert answers are useful only in so far as organizational problems are technical in nature – if the problem is based in human systems, then expert advice, no matter how prized, becomes only one of many perspectives on an issue. Most of the truly difficult problems in organizations fall in the latter category rather than the former, leaving organizations in a position that often feels too ambiguous for comfort. But it likewise leaves organizations with the possibility of an infinite number of answers. Those answers lie in the inventiveness of the organizational members, ordinary people who, working together, can generate workable answers to the problems of the organization.

Because there are many potential solutions, it is less critical that the collective come to a *right* answer and more critical that collective meaning is made, so that those who must act upon the meaning (and often that is everyone) can support their actions with their own reasoning. This is a substantially different concept from the familiar idea of including employees in a decision so that they will later support it. Organizational members *cannot* act responsibly except on the basis of their own conclusions – and to reach those conclusions they must participate in the creation of meaning.

5 Participant-generated database

Hallways are data rich. Participants bring into hallways the understanding they have gained about their own processes, about how they interact with other parts of the organization, and about what is important to them and what they value. They also bring data they have generated about their quality and data they have collected about their customers. Hallways bring together, not reports from others, but the *primary source* of the data, allowing the 'sense-making' process to be less inferential and more data-based. The data are publicly displayed in the hallway in charts, process maps, lists, plans and diagrams, so that each part of the organization knows what all other parts know – data are 'published' in the comprehensive meaning of that word. It is, however, not the data themselves, nor the sharing of them, but the *public discussion* that references that data and constructs meaning from them, that comprise the act of collective learning.

There are four critical data elements in hallways: the availability of organizational data; the primary source of the data being present; publishing the data, and the dialogue that constructs meaning from the data. These four elements highlight the difference between hallways and a more traditional organizational communication process in which learning is sometimes equated with sharing, or making public, organizational information.

6   Shared experience

Hallways function as a generative metaphor for the organization. Not only are hallways a source of new ideas for the organization, they are also a shared experience of interacting in new ways. Hallways, in many of their current forms, are temporary – organizational members know they will return to their normal way of relating and working at the end of the allotted time. However, if over time, organizational members have many experiences in which, as a collective, they are able to generate exciting new ideas, reframe issues in more useful ways, and act in a more egalitarian manner, they may come to think of themselves and others in a new light. The hallway may itself make another form of functioning seem more possible, more within reach.

Shared experiences are powerful sources of shared meaning, because it is possible to reference the experience and thus to bring to mind for everyone a meaningful image. In large organizations there are surprisingly few shared experiences. Organizations tend to hold meetings, training, retreats, etc. by organizational units or levels. Hallways can constitute a shared experience.

Having identified the characteristics of hallways it is also important to say what is not a hallway because organizations have many large and small group meetings that do not have these characteristics. Any meeting in which one or a few people make presentations or speeches to many is not a hallway – that would include most staff meetings and briefings. Q&A meetings where top management is answering the questions of employees, whether in person or through teleconferencing, are not hallways. Most management development programmes and professional conferences are not hallways. They are designed for individual learning but not for collective learning. Newsletters and reports that disseminate information are not hallways. All of these kinds of meetings may be necessary to the functioning of the organization, but they are not places in which collective learning can take place.

Unpredictable outcomes

When the six elements outlined above are designed into a hallway the meaning that the collective will construct is relatively unpredictable. That may be both the good and the bad news about hallways. The bad news is that because hallways require an investment of time and money, organizations may want some assurance that the outcomes will justify the cost outlay. Whether it is bringing 75 people together for the three days of a strategic search conference, holding two plus hours of appreciative interviews with every member of the organization, or having every team in the organization hold a discussion around a learning map, the investment is considerable and when organizations invest money, they like to know what they are getting.

The good news is that if the outcome were predictable organizations would not need intentionally to create hallways. It is the potential of the collective to create never-before-thought-of-meaning, to reframe problems in unexpected ways, and to uncover assumptions that the organization was not even aware were getting in the way, that make hallways so valuable. In human systems the price we pay for the almost limitless ability to construct our own future is that the future feels less like a linear progression and more chimerical.

Collective meaning versus group decisions

It is important to differentiate the making of collective meaning from group decision making. Hallways are about the former, not the latter. The intended outcome is a new way of understanding something that is shared across the collective. That new understanding may influence one or a multitude of decisions over time, but it is the shared understanding that is the goal. The meaning a collective constructs, and organizational decisions do not bear a one-to-one relationship with each other. Collective learning may result in an understanding that action should not be taken or organizational members may simply come away with a new perspective on an ambiguous issue.

Our negative fantasies and fears about creating hallways are more related to decisions than to the construction of collective meaning. What if organizational members make decisions that serve their own interests rather than the interests of the whole? What if no one takes responsibility? What if organizational members decide to do something that bankrupts the company? If I, as general manager, am going to be held responsible, how can I give up that much control? These are concerns about decision making, not about the construction of collective meaning.

Bohm (1990) relates a story about a North American Indian tribe of hunter-gatherers. From time to time the whole tribe would come together in a circle and talk. No one appeared to have called the meeting nor led it; the group made no decisions and seemingly had no agenda. Yet when the meeting ended people knew what to do because they now understood each other. They might then get together in small groups and make plans or decide to do something. Hallways produce a similar sense of knowing more about the whole and how the parts relate and therefore being able to act in concert with that shared understanding.

Summary

I want to return briefly to the description of how individuals learn (see Chapter 2) in order to establish a more explicit relationship between how individuals construct meaning in the process space of their minds and how collectives construct meaning in hallways. Chapter 2 described the way in which individuals relate new experiences to their existing meaning structures in a 'processing space' called working memory. This processing space is where the connections are built between ideas. When we say, 'I have been thinking about...' we are referring to the activity that goes on in that space. Having put ideas together in that processing space to construct new meaning for ourselves, we store that new meaning in long-term memory.

New experiences are critical for individual learning, but experience alone does not produce learning. It is the time we spend 'thinking about' or 'reflecting on' those experiences that creates the new meaning for us – the time we spend in that processing space. We have all known people about whom we would say, 'She never seems able to put two and two together' or 'Yes, he was involved, but he didn't seem to learn much from it'. We are saying, in effect, that the person did not actively or intentionally build the connections between ideas in the processing space of his or her mind.

Hallways are to collective learning what processing space is to individual learning. It is where ideas are connected and new ideas are constructed. Members of an organization are analogous to the eyes and ears of a person – the sensory organs – they bring to the organization many new experiences. But collective learning requires not just the new experiences, it also requires the processing space in which those members can connect the ideas they have with the ideas of others – the hallways. Hallways are essential to collective learning. They are not the only element that is required, as the next chapter will illustrate, but they are essential.

Let me build one further connection to individual learning.

Individuals do their processing – their putting together ideas to create new meaning – in many settings and under many different circumstances. As an individual you may do your thinking in the shower, and while you are commuting, as well as sitting at a desk with pencil in hand. You may set aside a period of time to 'go over' ideas and you may also find it facilitates your thinking to spend a brief period of time on an issue and then leave it alone for a while before returning to it. Most of us have developed multiple ways and times to build the connections among our ideas and experiences into meaning structures. We do not just 'think' on Tuesday afternoon at three o'clock, rather we have a wide variety of 'thinking' times and processes that we employ.

Likewise, organizations need many different kinds of hallways, not just one event or practice. Earlier I mentioned hallways such as Strategic Search Conferences, Open Space Technology, and Team Syntegrity. These are events, planned times for the organization to 'think'. But organizations also need everyday hallways, time analogous to the commuting or the shower. One way to encourage these more ongoing hallways is the arrangement of the physical space organizational members work in. Steelcase Corporation, itself an office furniture manufacturer, has created office areas that are designed as neighbourhoods'. Product and business teams that work together are located near each other in the neighbourhood and there is a community 'commons', where informal conversation and community interaction occur. Studies have shown that the availability of the 'commons' serves to significantly increase collaboration among team members (Wild, Bishop and Sullivan, 1996). The idea of pulsing between a 'personal harbour' where team members can focus on individual work and a 'commons' area designed for collaboration is, for many, the office design of the future.

Many other companies (e.g. Hitachi America Ltd, National City Bank, Owens Corning) have developed similar shared space, often with the design help of Steelcase. SAS Airlines in Stockholm has a 'central plaza' in the midst of its corporate headquarters. The plaza contains shops and a café where people from all levels and functions are encouraged to visit and share ideas – an ongoing hallway.

However, such hallways may raise concerns about whether individuals are using their time in the interest of the organization or whether they are just wasting it in office gossip. This was a concern for managers of a Siemens factory in North Carolina who had become aware of the amount of time that workers spent chatting in the cafeteria. There was talk about how to curb such an unproductive use of time, until a group of researchers from the Center for Workforce Development provided data about what was really happening in the cafeteria. The study showed that during a typical week more than 70 per cent of the 1000 workers who participated in the study said they shared information with co-workers while in the cafeteria, while 55 per cent said they asked co-workers for advice while there. The study convinced Siemens' management that they ought to be facilitating these conversations rather than hindering them. As a result they placed empty pads of paper and overhead projectors in the cafeteria to facilitate informal meetings.

Like Siemens there are many ways an organization can facilitate naturally occurring hallways. Many Japanese companies have 'talk rooms'. At Dai-Ichi Pharmaceuticals researchers are expected to visit the 'talk room' daily to discuss their current work. These discussions occur with whom ever they find there, random conversations that build the critical connections between ideas. Davenport and Prusak (1998) describe this phenomenon as '. . . a kind of Brownian motion theory of knowledge exchange, its very randomness encouraging the discovery of new ideas that a more specifically directed discussion would miss' (p. 92).

Organizations increasingly faced with unique and ambiguous issues are finding a rich resource in the collective learning of their members. However, to tap into that resource they are having to create new processes that are strikingly different from the ways they have interacted in the past. The many new forms of hallways are meeting that need.

References

Argyris, C. and Schon, D. A. (1978). *Organizational Learning: A Theory of Action Perspective*. Reading MA: Addison-Wesley.

Beer, S. (1994). *Beyond Dispute: The Invention of Team Syntegrity*. New York: Wiley.

Bohm, D. (1990). 'On dialogue' (transcript). Ojai CA: David Bohm Seminars.

Bolman, L. G. and Deal, T. E. (1991). *Reframing Organizations: Artistry, Choice, and Leadership*. San Francisco: Jossey-Bass.

Cooperrider, D. (1995). 'An Interview with David Cooperrider on Appreciative Inquiry and the Future of OD'. *Organization Development Journal*, **13** (3), 5–13.

Davenport, T. H. and Prusak, L. (1998). *Working Knowledge: How Organizations Manage What they Know*. Boston: Harvard Business School Press.

Emery, M. (ed.) (1993). *Participative Design for Participative Democracy*. Centre for Continuing Education, Australian National University.

Jacobs, R. (1994). *Real Time Strategic Change*. San Francisco: Berrett-Kohler.

McClellan, J. (1983). 'Toward a general model of collective learning: A critique of existing models of specific social systems and a sketch of a model for social systems in general', unpublished dissertation, University of Massachusetts.

Owen, H. (1991). *Riding the Tiger: Doing Business in a Transforming World*. Potomac, MD, Abbott Publishing.

Revans, R. (1983). *ABC of Action Learning*. England: Chartwell-Bratt Ltd. Perrysburg, Ohio: Root Learning Inc.

Schwartz, P. (1991). *The Art of the Long View: Planning For the Future in an Uncertain World*. New York: Doubleday.

Weick, K. (1995). *Sensemaking in Organizations*. Thousand Oaks CA: Sage.

Weisbord, M. (1992). *Discovering Common Ground*. San Francisco: Berrett-Kohler.

Wild, H., Bishop, L. and Sullivan, C. L. (1996). *Building environments for learning and innovation*. Menlo Park CA: Institute for Research on Learning.

4 The organizational learning cycle

For organizational learning to occur it is not enough simply to encourage organizational members to exchange their accessible meaning structures with each other – the organization must actively facilitate collective learning. In this chapter I describe an organizational learning cycle that involves four steps:

1 Widespread generation of information.
2 Integration of new/local information into the organizational context.
3 Collective interpretation of information.
4 Having authority to take responsible action based on the interpreted meaning.

Four steps

The four steps are circular in that the fourth step, having authority to take responsible action on the interpreted meaning,

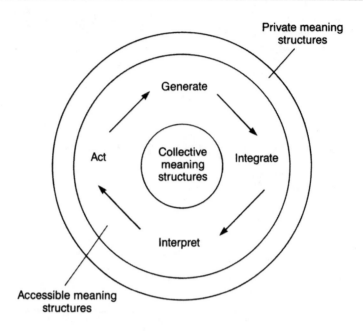

Figure 4.1   The organizational learning cycle

generates yet more information and begins the cycle again (see Figure 4.1).

The steps of generating, integrating, interpreting and acting on information are not new to organizations. However, organizations typically carry out these steps in ways that severely limit organizational learning. Typically, a different part of the organization conducts each step. For example, the Marketing department often assumes responsibility for collecting external information, Research and Development is responsible for generating new ideas and products, MIS is tasked with the distribution of information within the organization, the interpretation of information is accomplished by top management, and those who take action based on the interpretation are often at lower levels in the organization far removed from those who made the interpretation. When the steps of the organizational learning cycle are disconnected, collective learning is lost. If we want organizational learning to occur, then we must make drastic changes in the way these four steps are undertaken as well as who accomplishes them. The organizational members who generate the data will need to be involved in the interpretation, but not without understanding the context in which it exists, which means having a more complete picture of the organization. The organizational members who make the interpretation need also to be the ones to act on it in order to learn the extent to which their interpretation made sense and what additional data are needed to make a better interpretation.

It may be helpful to relate the organizational learning cycle to Kolb's (1984) experiential learning cycle which was summarized in Chapter 2. For organizational learning to occur, each member of the organization must still engage in all the steps of the experiential learning cycle. But a great deal more must transpire to create collective, rather than just individual, learning. Figure 4.2 relates the steps in the organizational learning cycle to the experiential learning cycle.

In Kolb's model the individual engages in a concrete experience; at the collective level it is necessary that all organizational

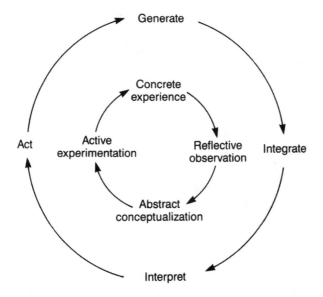

Figure 4.2 The organizational learning cycle and the experiential learning cycle

members engage in the practices that gather information from the external environment (customers, suppliers, conferences) and that likewise all engage in work-related experiments that produce new information. In Kolb's model the second step is reflective observation: the individual reflects on an experience, recalling what was notable, or, to use the language of Chapter 2, what was different. Again, at the collective level, the task is more complex: everyone needs all of the information everyone else has. The task is one of integrating newly generated information into the organizational context. The third step in Kolb's model is abstract conceptualization. The individual draws conclusions about the experience, but in organizational learning the task of interpreting information is a collective one. Organizational members come to the task with different perspectives, and therefore different ways of interpreting the information. Those differences are critical to the organizational learning process: without difference learning does not occur. Finally, in Kolb's model the individual is able to test out the conclusions that he or she has reached through active experimentation. Likewise, for collective learning, organizational members must act on the collective interpretation they have made. Action serves both to test the interpretation and to generate new information to continue the learning.

Before describing these four steps in detail, I want to provide three case examples of organizational learning. These examples illustrate the variety of ways organizations have implemented the basic steps of the organizational learning cycle. All of these organizations are self-proclaimed learning organizations and have been extensively written about in the literature as such.

However, I want to share with the reader the hesitancy I have about offering case examples. One difficulty is how to offer illustrations without implying a causal relationship. All of these organizations are successful, or were at the time of their reports; however, we have no way of knowing the extent to which that success is a result of the organizational learning processes that they have implemented. These organizations were involved in many other initiatives at the same time as they were implementing processes related to learning, and those initiatives or even just the general circumstances at the time may well have affected their performance as much as the learning processes themselves. Moreover, it is conceivable that an organization could implement all of the steps of the organizational learning cycle and still fail because the organization simply had a poor product or service, the market was too fragmented, the organization was under-capitalized, or because of a hundred other factors unrelated to organizational learning.

Even if we wanted to make a claim about the relationship between organizational learning and success, we would first have to agree upon what success was. The success of the World Health Organization, one of the examples, is of a considerably different nature from the success of another example, Chaparral Steel. The definition of organizational learning offered earlier (the intentional use of learning processes at the individual, group and system level to continuously transform the organization in a direction that is increasingly satisfying to its stakeholders) does not necessarily imply financial success.

A second concern I have in offering case examples is that they are primarily, although not exclusively, taken from the organizational literature. There is a tendency for journal articles to be promotional; most tend to build a case for the success of the organization as well as for the processes that were used to achieve that success. We rarely get a balanced picture that incorporates a sense of the problems that the organization had in implementing the processes or any new problems that might have resulted from the implementation. We also lack understanding of the tacit knowledge that was necessary to the implementation of these processes: most of what we read about are explicit actions.

Finally, I would be violating the principles I have articulated in this book if I were to say, 'Here is how to do it: simply copy WHO or do it the way Chaparral or Johnsonville Foods does'. I believe each organization must use its own learning capacity to invent the specific processes it needs for organizational learning.

Having made so many caveats the reader may wonder why the case examples are here at all. They are here because I believe they are useful in illustrating the wide variety of ways the steps of the organizational learning cycle might be implemented. I have selected the examples on the basis of variety, although all of them are in relatively small organizations, particularly compared with most *Fortune 500* companies. The variety lends credence to the idea that we can learn for ourselves the way to implement the basic principles. I would hope the cases would be viewed as a source of ideas, but not as answers.

In the end, perhaps, the examples are most useful in helping us see that something is possible. It is always difficult to put our energies into learning how to do something until we believe it can be done.

Chaparral Steel

Chaparral Steel is a minimill in Midlothian, Texas. It is the tenth largest US steel producer, with sales over $400 million. Chaparral has taken as its goal to lead the world in the low-cost, safe production of high-quality steel. Much of the success of Chaparral can be attributed to a culture that is focused on learning. It is, however, important to place that culture within the context of the industry.

In the 1950s the US steel industry contained a small number of fully integrated steel manufacturers. Firms typically owned iron and coal mines, railroads to transport the raw materials to the mills, and trucks to deliver the finished products to the customers. There was little or no foreign competition and the major competitive factor among US companies was price, with little differentiation in type of product. Under these circumstances US steel makers devoted little effort to research and development or even to plant modernization. When US labour costs rose in the 1970s, foreign competitors, who had rebuilt their mills with the latest technology after the Second World War, proved too much for these large integrated mills, many of which declared bankruptcy.

Minimills began to emerge in the mid-1970s. They had approximately 6 per cent of the market in 1975, and that had increased to 26 per cent by 1990. The minimills are tech-nology driven, mostly non-unionized and are focused on quality speciality products, such as reinforcing bars, beams, angles and large rounds. Where the larger mills were fully integrated, the minimills recycled scrap. When Chaparral began production of steel in 1975 there were fewer than a dozen minimills; by the mid-1980s there were 60. Chaparral's most challenging competi-tion has come from Third World companies that pay employees as little as $2.30 an hour. In order to compete in this fast growing market Chaparral has had to steadily reduce the number of hours needed to produce a ton of steel. Currently Chaparral produces steel at 1.3 hours per ton, against an industry average of 10 hours per ton. The steel business has traditionally been labour-intensive, capital-intensive and energy-intensive. To compete, Chaparral needed to enlist the aid of its employees to design those elements out of the production process.

Chaparral considers itself a 'Learning Lab' and has some straightforward principles that it uses to reach its competitive goals: (1) owning the problem and solving it, (2) garnering and integrating knowledge, and (3) challenging the *status quo*. The principles are ones that many organizations strive to put into place. Chaparral has been able to make them work, in part, because they are accomplished within a culture based on the belief that human nature is inherently good, energetic, creative and trustworthy. There is an overriding belief in the power of the human mind to invent and create. Chaparral has had the advantage of being a greenfield site and thus hiring employees with the principles and beliefs in mind. In fact, an early employ-ment policy was to avoid potential staff who had worked in the steel industry and thus might have learned practices anti-thetical to the ones Chaparral was using.

Owning the problem and solving it

Because of an unambiguous mission which is translatable into operational objectives, employees are given discretion both to identify and to solve problems independently. The norm is: if you have a good idea, act on it. This means that 90 per cent of the problems never make it to a morning meeting but are solved on the spot, often by spontaneous meetings of those involved in the problem. The downside of this flexibility is that engineers, who might have a better way to address problems, are often not called.

The willingness to own and solve problems is fostered by an egalitarianism. There are no status symbols like assigned parking or separate dining areas at Chaparral. Operators are not assigned to shifts by seniority; rather everyone rotates onto night shift, ensuring that knowledge is spread across shifts. There are no hourly wage earners, everyone is paid a salary, and of course no time clocks. There is a 'no fault' approach to sickness and absenteeism and no reporting structure to track individual employees' absenteeism, yet overall employee absenteeism is less than 1 per cent. Bonus systems are linked to company profits, 8.5 per cent of the gross profit before taxes. Ninety-three per cent of employees are stockholders. Chaparral is a flat organization with only two levels between the CEO and the operators in the mill.

Garnering and integrating knowledge

This principle is operationalized by employees every day, in every project, adding to the knowledge resources. Employees use the steel process itself as an analogy to talk about an 'unimpeded flow of information' rather than 'batch-processed information'. This flow is aided by Chaparral's size, which is deliberately held to under a thousand employees. The building structure is also deliberately designed to enhance the flow of information: for example, the locker room is located in the headquarters building so employees pass through at least twice a day. The building design provides many opportunities for members to have accidental and frequent meetings. Work is also structured with the objective of disseminating knowledge. For example, the initial team on a new process is, subsequently, deliberately dispersed among the rest of the crews to diffuse the knowledge.

There is an emphasis on multi-skilling and multi-functioning. For example, everyone is considered a salesperson and has a business card to use with customers. Security guards do data entry while on night duty. Fork-lift operators do their own routine maintenance. Janitors are able to enter customer orders into the system. Sales, billing, credit and shipping are all housed under the same roof and employees are cross-trained to be able to perform each other's functions. If a customer calls shipping, that person can also answer billing or credit questions. Likewise there are few staff positions: typical staff functions such as hiring, safety, training and MIS reside within line departments. This multi-functioning not only makes the organization more flexible, it also reduces territorial possessiveness over information. The pay structure rewards the accumulation of skills as well as performance.

A critical element for learning is the integration of research and development with production; development takes place on the floor. There is no separate R&D department: the lab is the plant. There are, at times, miniature models of equipment on the factory floor that allow workers to try out new processes or procedures before engaging the expensive full-size equipment. This facilitates 'what if' thinking that might not even be considered without this 'thinking aid'. The people who make the steel are responsible for keeping their process on the leading edge of technology. All employees consider themselves to be part of research and development. For example, two maintenance workers invented a machine for strapping bundles of steel rods together that reduced the cost from $250 000 to $60 000 and was faster and more flexible.

The focus on innovation goes beyond the factory floor. For example, on a Monday morning in Los Angeles a customer suggested to a Chaparral representative that he would buy more steel if minor modifications were made in the size and shape of a particular product. On Monday afternoon those changes were discussed in a production meeting at the plant in Midlothian, Texas. A decision was made to meet the customer's specifications and by Wednesday the new product was being produced. Within two weeks of the initial request the product was being delivered.

Winning as a company takes precedence over individual ownership of ideas. The belief is that ideas go through a gestation period where lots of people figure out how to make the idea work. Individuals are not singled out for praise because of the belief that if individuals are singled out they will begin to protect good ideas. The result is that Chaparral employees are often unable to identify the source of production innovation – the reward for having ideas is getting to carry them out. But neither are they singled out for blame. There is an absence of punitive actions following failures. Mistakes are considered a normal part of risk taking and as important learning opportunities.

Chaparral invests heavily in training of all kinds but places particular emphasis on their apprenticeship programme which was developed in collaboration with the US Department of Labor's Bureau of Apprenticeship and Training. The three-and-a-half year apprenticeship programme allows employees to reach the level of senior operator after 7280 hours of on-the-job training and formal schooling. Selected foremen rotate in from the floor to teach the formal part of the programme, teaching such topics as metallurgy, basic mechanical maintenance, basic engineering, and ladder logic programming. The philosophy of the programme is stated as 'It is the intent of Chaparral Steel to provide the broadest possible growth experience for every person employed by the company. We believe that the company grows in excellence in direct proportion to the growth of its people' (Chaparral Steel, 1987, p. 10). Ninety per cent of employees participate in some form of training programme. Much of the learning is conducted on the job or through cross-training, but even so, employees average four hours per week in a classroom. This figure is in sharp contrast to national statistics which reveal that training is primarily offered to managers, with nationally less than 30 per cent of line workers receiving job training. There is a sabbatical plan for front-line supervisors at Chaparral. Chaparral discovered that supervisors typically stay engaged for about three years and then tend to get bored with the job. Supervisors are sent on sabbatical to do special projects and while they are gone others are put in place as substitutes. Chaparral calls this 'vice-ing'. Substitutes often break the productivity records of absent supervisors, giving them something to shoot for when they return. Sabbatical projects might include visiting other steel mills, spending time with customers, or looking into new equipment or programmes under consideration.

Challenging the 'status quo'

Chaparral selects employees for their desire to challenge their own and others' thinking. They look for innovators and for individuals with a positive attitude toward learning. Gordon Forward, president and CEO, says, 'We're looking for managers who can do more than just run the company. They must improve it. If all we wanted to do was run this plant, we could get rid of the kind of people we have – the kind who never leave it alone' (Chaparral Steel, 1987, p. 15). Typically eight applicants are interviewed for each one granted a second interview, which takes place in the prospective department. The second interview lasts most of a day and is held not only with the immediate supervisor but with members of the work group.

Large and small experiments are continually being conducted. Line managers can authorize tens of thousands of dollars for experiments without higher authority. An example of this experimentation is setting goals beyond current production capabilities. Howard Duff, General Manager, in explaining why a particular product was being developed says, 'We decided on the twenty-four-inch because we wanted to explore the most technically challenging product. Because there may be some idiosyncrasies about the process that we need to learn...' (Leonard-Barton, 1992, p. 25).

Employees scan the world for technical expertise that others have created. They benchmark against best-of-class companies, even from totally different industries. Believing that by the time they hear about an innovation at a conference it will be too late, Chaparral has developed an extensive network to gain early access to new ideas. Multi-level teams visit universities, maintain long-term relationships with suppliers, and visit competitors. Chaparral invests heavily in employee travel for benchmarking or to investigate a new technology. Teams have been sent to Japan, Sweden and West Germany to investigate what other industries have to offer. Knowledge does not need to filter down because the people who gather the information are the same people who will use it.

While functioning like a learning laboratory Chaparral has set world records for monthly tonnage. By 1984 the company was listed in *Fortune* as one of the ten best-managed factories in the US. Chaparral put out 1000 tons of steel per worker-year in 1989, compared with the US average of 350 tons and the Japanese average of 600 tons. Chaparral's profit margin is 11 per cent of sales compared with an industry average of 6 per cent. Employee turnover is less than 2 per cent per quarter compared with the 10 per cent US manufacturing average. Among the indicators of which Chaparral is most proud is being the only US steelmaker to be awarded the Japanese Industrial Standard certification in 1989.

In Figure 4.3 I have extrapolated some of the learning initiatives at Chaparral Steel and placed them within the four steps of the organizational learning cycle. In so doing it is evident that some of what Chaparral has been involved in is not represented in the figure. Yet it is equally clear that Chaparral is heavily investing in each of the steps of the organizational learning cycle.

In the first step, widespread generation of information, Chaparral has certainly excelled. There are concerted efforts to involve every member of the organization in collecting information to bring into the organization: the field visits made by multi-functional teams and the intentional fostering of networks to gain early access to new technology. Even the sabbatical plan for supervisors seems designed to give employees first-hand experience.

Chaparral has done an equally good job of involving everyone in the generation of new internal information. Thinking of the factory floor as a learning lab epitomizes that attitude. The resource allocation of $10 000 for experimentation, the integration of R&D and production, and hiring based on learning potential are all effective ways to implement the generation of new information.

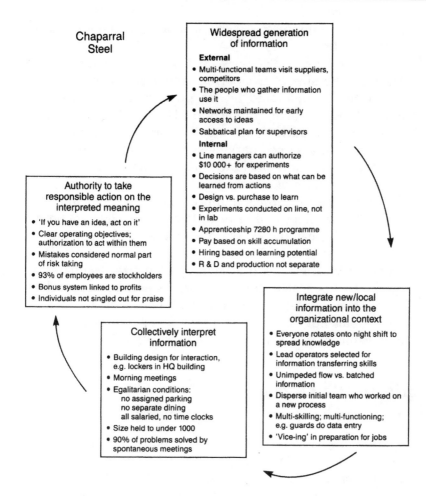

Chaparral Steel

Widespread generation of information

External
- Multi-functional teams visit suppliers, competitors
- The people who gather information use it
- Networks maintained for early access to ideas
- Sabbatical plan for supervisors

Internal
- Line managers can authorize $10 000+ for experiments
- Decisions are based on what can be learned from actions
- Design vs. purchase to learn
- Experiments conducted on line, not in lab
- Apprenticeship 7280 h programme
- Pay based on skill accumulation
- Hiring based on learning potential
- R & D and production not separate

Authority to take responsible action on the interpreted meaning
- 'If you have an idea, act on it'
- Clear operating objectives; authorization to act within them
- Mistakes considered normal part of risk taking
- 93% of employees are stockholders
- Bonus system linked to profits
- Individuals not singled out for praise

Integrate new/local information into the organizational context
- Everyone rotates onto night shift to spread knowledge
- Lead operators selected for information transferring skills
- Unimpeded flow vs. batched information
- Disperse initial team who worked on a new process
- Multi-skilling; multi-functioning; e.g. guards do data entry
- 'Vice-ing' in preparation for jobs

Collectively interpret information
- Building design for interaction, e.g. lockers in HQ building
- Morning meetings
- Egalitarian conditions:
  no assigned parking
  no separate dining
  all salaried, no time clocks
- Size held to under 1000
- 90% of problems solved by spontaneous meetings

Figure 4.3   The organizational learning cycle for Chaparral Steel

The second step of the organizational learning cycle, integrating new/local information into the organizational context, is again accomplished by a number of processes: the multi-skilling and multi-functioning that occurs, the dispersal of initial teams so that their new knowledge is spread and the rotating shifts. Factory workers who consider themselves salespersons must certainly have a broader understanding of the organization into which to position the information they are generating.

Perhaps most impressive is the metaphor of an unimpeded flow of information.

The third step, collectively interpreting information, is facilitated by the size of Chaparral, which is deliberately held to under 1000 people, and by the physical design of space that encourages frequent interaction. The egalitarian conditions, which include such things as all salaried employees, no time clocks and no assigned parking spaces, create a climate in which employees are more likely to challenge and question. Much of the interpretation of information at Chaparral appears to go on in spontaneous meetings that occur when a problem arises.

The fourth step, authority to take responsible action on the interpreted meaning, grows out of the third step: those who meet to solve the problem then act on the interpretation they have made. The reward system of Chaparral facilitates action by the bonus system linked to profits and by the stockholder plan. There appears to be a thoughtful norm about not singling individuals out for praise in a way that would discourage joint ownership of problems and solutions.

World Health Organization

In 1966 the World Health Organization (WHO) established a goal to rid the Earth of smallpox. Before its eradication 10 million people a year were inflicted with the disease. Smallpox spreads by minute droplets that are discharged from the mouth and nose of infected victims. About 10–15 days after inhaling the virus the infected person becomes sick with a high fever and flu-like symptoms. A rash appears on the face and within a day or two spreads over the entire body. The pimple-like papules become enlarged and by the fifth day are filled with pus. By the tenth day scabs begin to form, and then fall off by the third week, leaving pitted scars. Once smallpox has been contracted there is no effective treatment. Between 20 and 40 per cent of those infected die, and those recovering are left scarred and sometimes blind. The disease can be transmitted from the time the rash appears to the time the scabs drop off, a period of about four weeks.

The decision to wage the 1966 campaign was not simply a response to new technology. A smallpox vaccine had been available for several decades before. In fact, a similar campaign, although not carried out, had been proposed to the League of Nations as early as 1926. By 1966 the widespread use of the vaccine in North America and Western Europe had virtually eliminated smallpox from those areas, except for occasional outbreaks resulting from importation.

The guiding strategy of the WHO for the elimination of smallpox was to conduct mass vaccination in the 30 countries where smallpox was epidemic. In 1966 past experience in epidemiology overwhelmingly indicated that the most successful strategy was surveillance and control. The WHO, however, chose mass vaccination, a strategy that involves immunizing 80 per cent of the population on the supposition that smallpox would then decline more or less automatically. The choice of mass vaccination over surveillance and control was influenced by the effectiveness of a test conducted in 1963 on the island of Tonga. Through hindsight it is possible to see that a strategy that was effective in an isolated and remote location might not be transferable to more contiguous areas; however, at the time the mass vaccination strategy appeared well based and sound.

The mass vaccination strategy was employed from the initiation of the campaign until it finally came into question following a smallpox outbreak in eastern Nigeria, an area where 90 per cent of the population had already been vaccinated. Delay in the delivery of supplies to the Nigerian area necessitated a temporary change in strategy. With only a limited amount of vaccine available, new smallpox cases were searched out and vaccinations were given in the immediate geographical area surrounding each case. By the time the mass-campaign supplies arrived a few months later, there were no detectable cases in eastern Nigeria. The containment strategy had worked.

As a result of the Nigeria experience and several other similar experiences, the worldwide strategy was changed to surveillance–containment. This strategy, which was whimsically called

' "The Bank Robber Theory" – go where the money is', involved discovering new outbreaks before the smallpox had time to spread, then vaccinating the victims' families, neighbours, and then the village, in an ever-widening circle until no more cases occurred. Using this strategy it was discovered that smallpox could be contained even when only 50 per cent of the population was vaccinated. Ultimately, the surveillance and containment strategy proved itself successful in the worldwide campaign. It is to the credit of the WHO that rather than defending its initial strategy, the organization was able to interpret the data and reframe the strategy.

Over time the WHO came to realize that its initial estimates of the amount of vaccine needed, the incident rate and the morbidity rate, to name only a few of the factors, were woefully inaccurate and underestimated, in some cases by a factor of 40. Thus, the problem, as initially defined, was inaccurate. It was the organization's ability to learn that permitted the WHO to redefine problems repeatedly and thereby make the major shifts in strategy necessary to combat the disease.

The method of vaccination is another example of change in strategy. Traditionally smallpox vaccination had been given by the scratch method, in which a drop of vaccine was placed on the skin and then scratched into the superficial layers. The WHO decided to use the jet injector, which had recently been invented by the US military. The jet injector was an improvement both because it used less vaccine and because it could provide a standard dosage and could therefore be used by relatively untrained personnel. Perhaps most influential in this decision was that the jet injector represented the latest technology – it was capable of handling up to 1000 vaccinations an hour. Over time, fieldworkers realized that speed had little advantage in a campaign that was more likely to advance from house to house or occur while standing by the town well. The jet injector also presented ongoing problems of cost and maintenance. The bifurcated needle which eventually replaced it was almost primitive by contrast. It allowed a single drop of vaccine to flow between two needles placed like the tines of a fork. The bifurcated needle could be boiled or flamed with a match over

200 times without dulling. Thus it was more field-worthy, if less high-tech. By 1969 the bifurcated needle was being used worldwide. Again WHO was able to learn through its field experience rather than defend its original choice.

Early on, WHO recognized the need to learn constantly from the fieldworkers' experience and to adapt and change accordingly. Although policies were established centrally, control resided at the local level. Thus fieldworkers were able to alter their vaccination processes in keeping with the local culture. In locations where tattooing was used to ward off witchcraft, the vaccination scar became a part of that custom. In some areas midwives were used to encourage vaccination, in others the scar was a sign of the independence of that country, in others radio was used as a major tool, and in yet others, nomads were vaccinated when they arrived at the public water-hole. This variation was systematically recorded and religiously made available to other fieldworkers. Every two to three weeks a summary of the status of the programme with findings and new approaches appeared in WHO's *Weekly Epidemiological Record*. Special papers on operational methods and results of research appeared with equal frequency. Requests for help from the field were treated by the central office with absolute priority and were given immediate response. In addition to yearly regional meetings, all headquarters staff and regional advisors were expected to spend at least one-third of their time in the field, visiting each country at least once and preferably twice a year.

The variation in practice and the emphasis on collecting and sharing findings allowed WHO to innovate and learn continuously. The organization learned that even the most longstanding techniques should be questioned. For example, through analysis of the data it was discovered that the time honoured technique of swabbing the vaccination site made no significant difference in bacterial infection; thus costly supplies were eliminated and time was reduced. Through close analysis of the data it was learned that adult women rarely contracted smallpox and thus did not need to be vaccinated; likewise, 95 per cent of the cases occurred in people who had never been vaccinated, so revaccination could be eliminated.

These findings were possible because of the attention WHO gave to the collection of data and perhaps even more because of the type of data WHO chose to collect. It would have advantaged WHO politically to track the number of vaccinations given and the number of areas which were free from smallpox. WHO chose, however, to track trends in the *incidence* of smallpox. Although those data frequently proved embarrassing both to WHO and to the countries in which the cases were reported, it allowed WHO to learn in a way that would not have been possible from data that was more sensitive to public relations. Negative as well as positive results were widely publicized. All data were scrutinized for age, sex, vaccination status and geographic distribution of cases so that use of resources could be maximized.

Considerable attention was given to improving reporting. In some countries a reward was offered to the first person in an area who reported an undiscovered outbreak to authorities. The rewards were large, sometimes equivalent to one month's income for poor villagers. A manual was produced detailing the philosophy of surveillance and outlining methods for improving case detection and notification. A major breakthrough in reporting occurred when each local unit began to be visited regularly by a mobile surveillance team who provided instruction and assistance. The fact that someone was actively and visibly concerned with receiving reports and then acted on those reports encouraged increased reporting.

In 1975, H. Mahler, then Director-General of the WHO said, 'It is the beginning of the end for smallpox, which can never return to ravage the earth as in centuries past. But it is also the beginning of a new era for WHO, which – having shown what can be done to eliminate disease when all nations join together in a unified, coordinated effort – can now attack more effectively the multitude of other major health problems still confronting us' (Mahler, 1975, p. 3).

Thus the organizational learning that WHO accomplished not only eradicated smallpox, it resulted in improved national reporting systems for communicable diseases, better techniques

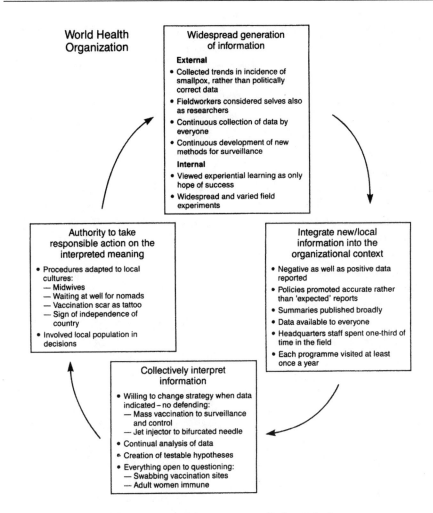

Figure 4.4   The organizational learning cycle for WHO

for immunization, and more sophisticated communicable disease control services.

The eradication of smallpox was the first global eradication of a major disease. The last case of smallpox occurred in Somalia in 1977.

Figure 4.4 places the initiatives of the World Health Organization within the organizational learning cycle. The first step, the widespread generation of information, was strongly supported by WHO both internally and externally. In particular, the choice of the type of data to collect was significant. Everyone involved in the campaign seemed to feel a responsibility to collect the data that was key to WHO's learning. Like Chaparral, WHO was able to select its employees with learning in mind. Field-workers constantly experimented with new processes and techniques. They saw themselves as researchers, not just as dispensers of vaccine.

The second step of the organizational learning cycle, integrating new/local information into the organizational context, reflected a dedication to full and open disclosure of all information. This was accomplished not only through the many reports that were widely circulated, but also by the many field visits of headquarters staff. Fieldworkers had available to them everything that was going on everywhere else: both what was working and what was failing.

The third step, collectively interpreting information, reflects the careful analysis of both statistical and anecdotal data, which was ongoing. The norm of considering everything open to question, even such long-standing traditions as swabbing vaccination sites, served WHO well.

The fourth step, authority to take responsible action on the interpreted meaning, was where WHO excelled. The field-workers had authority to act on what they were learning from the data. They were able to vary their practice by local conditions and to involve the local population in those decisions. Control at the local level was not only a necessity to accomplish the task, but also proved a way to enhance the learning. WHO provides an excellent example of how responsible action can lead to the generation of new information.

Johnsonville Foods

Johnsonville Foods was started in 1945 as a sausage company by the Stayer family in a small town in Wisconsin, Johnsonville.

In 1968, when the Stayers' son, Ralph, returned from Yale, the sausage company employed 12 people. By 1980, Johnsonville Foods was a very profitable $15 million turnover company that sold its sausage in five states and employed about 200 people.

In the early 1980s Ralph Stayer, now CEO, decided that the organization needed to change. It was profitable and still growing at a rate of 20 per cent annually, but it concerned Stayer that employees did not seem to care: they seemed bored and uninterested in their own performance. They made mistakes, that, while not deliberate, reflected a lack of responsibility – things like driving the prongs of a forklift through a newly built wall, adding the wrong seasonings to a sausage mix, or spraying a batch of sausage with water while cleaning the area. On the other hand he noticed that employees were leading vital lives outside of the organization as active community members involved in scouting and other responsible positions. It worried Stayer that they did not bring this same energy to their jobs.

Stayer was also concerned about competition, both regionally and nationally. National competitors were certainly capable of out-promoting and underpricing a small company like Johnsonville Foods. The regional competitors, of which there were several, could potentially provide better service to customers. Given the uninterested attitude of Johnsonville employees it was difficult to see how the company could survive any serious competitive challenge.

Stayer first looked to the management literature for answers. Finding none that seemed suited to his situation, he determined that he would have to come up with the answers on his own; after all, he concluded, he had, by his own management style, created the situation in which employees were uninterested – he would have to fix it as well.

Stayer's early efforts were to increase communication. He held what came to be known as 4:1s because he often met groups of four people to discuss what they wanted the organization to become. Later the 4:1s became fireside chats that involved 20–25 people. The CEO and other top administrators would articulate their vision for change and they would listen to the concerns of the employees. During this time Stayer's intent was to construct a company goal and then to motivate others to commit to it. What Stayer found over time was that this process did not work: nothing much changed. Stayer came to believe that he had little direct control over the performance of those who reported to him.

The answer, as he began to conceive it, was to create an organisation in which people were responsible for their own performance. The metaphor he conceived was a flock of geese on the wing. The geese, he surmised, have a common goal. Each takes turns leading, and most importantly, each of the geese is responsible for its own performance.

People becoming responsible for their own performance, Stayer believed, would take a fundamental shift in the mind set of everyone, including himself. In several journal articles Stayer has chronicled his own struggle to give up power (Stayer, 1990; Brokaw and Hartman, 1990). He came to believe that he had to change, a process he found difficult but rewarding. Responsibility meant that employees needed to be the owners of the problems, which included the power to make decisions related to the problems as well as having all of the information necessary to make the decisions. As an example of that responsibility, prior to the changeover the senior management team met several times a week to evaluate the product; they checked it for taste, colour and texture. As employees assumed more responsibility, the employees themselves did the tasting, but also were given the responsibility to make the changes necessary to improve what went wrong. Employees began to ask for more information on customer reaction, costs, efficiency and yield – data they needed to make the decisions. Information systems had to be redesigned to give them what they needed when they needed it. Increasingly, the information was collected, generated and used by employees themselves with no intermediaries to control the flow. For example, complaint letters from customers began going directly to the line, to address and when necessary to respond to customers. Stayer notes 'There is a lot of talk about making people feel important. I don't agree with that. I think we have to make people *be* important – and know it' (Brokaw and Hartman, 1990, p. 50).

The changeover was accomplished by making major revisions in four pivotal and interrelated systems of the organization: performance management, information/feedback, reward and people.

Performance management system

Before the 1980s good performance at Johnsonville was, as in most companies, defined by management. The change was to have those who actually do the work define and measure their own performance. Stayer came to believe that 'the real role of the CEO is to generate productive conversations about what performance ought to look like' (Brokaw and Hartman, 1990, p. 50). Thus the new performance system was to be designed from the customer's perspective. The question members were asked to address was: 'For your specific product or service what does great performance look like to the customer?'. Teams who shared a task went to their customers, whether external or internal, to ask that question and then wrestled with how to get those answers down on paper in a way that identified specific results that were measurable. Management set general parameters for budget and production and members were responsible for meeting the standards they had identified within those parameters. Members were, as well, responsible for measuring their performance, which required changes in the second system, information.

Information system

When the performance standards had been identified by the members who actually did the task, Management Information Systems, whose name was changed to Member Information Systems, was asked by the members for assistance in finding ways to generate real-time measures that would allow them to determine how well they were doing and where the problems were. These measures needed to be in a format that was usable to the members themselves. That system then became the way to get continuous improvement, but was also tied to the third system, rewards.

Reward system

Before the change, Johnsonville gave employees two bonuses a year, one before the busy summer season began and one when it was over, as a reward for their hard work. The bonuses rewarded everyone equally regardless of their performance. Recognizing that the old system did not fit the new mind set, Stayer eliminated the bonuses and in their place outlined a new system based on increased responsibility and performance. The new system, however, proved little better than the former system, because it relied on supervisors to identify good performers, a nearly impossible task when supervisors had become coaches of up to 50 members – supervisors simply did not know enough about each individual's performance to make the new system fair and equitable. The reward system was revised once again, but this time by a team of members themselves. The new system rewarded performers based on individual job performance, performance as a team member and personal growth and development. The system was designed and administered by a volunteer team of line production workers from various departments. Twice a year members share a percentage of the company's profit.

People system

What was required was 'to change the focus of the company from using people to build a great business to using the business to build great people' (Honald, 1991, p. 56). An important way the shift was symbolized was no longer to use the term employee (which the dictionary defines as being used for wages) and instead to refer to everyone in the organization as a member.

The people system involves recruiting the right people, developing them, and retaining them. New members are recruited on the basis of their willingness to learn as well as their performance capability. Members became convinced that performance problems resulted from the poor selection of new employees. They ask to be involved in the selection process as well. Selection procedures were established which line workers were able both to follow and eventually to improve. Line workers gradually took over most of the traditional personnel functions. Current members play a major role in the orientation and training of the new members, under the adage that what you teach you learn twice. However, once orientated and trained, members become responsible for their own development. Human Resource Development, now called Member Development, provides the resources to help members determine what they need and to resource those needs, but the responsibility remains with the members themselves. One resource provided is a development fund that sets aside $100 for each member of the company to spend every year on any development activity he or she chooses, which ranges from buying books to attending industry training. Another programme gives any member the opportunity to spend a day with any other member to get a better idea of what the other member's job entails. An extensive e-mail system allows members to share their successes with each other.

The third element of the people system is retention, the goal of which is to assist members who are performing below standard to improve. It is again managed by the members themselves. Any member who is functioning below acceptable levels is coached by other team members who make a contract with the low-performing employee for improvement. Within a well-defined process, teams monitor, correct and, if necessary, even fire their own members.

The initial emphasis on learning was viewed as negative by some organizational members: they felt that learning was personal and not the company's business. Over time, members began to see the connection between learning and their performance and over 65 per cent of the members became involved in some kind of formal education programme. Learning is seen as the acquisition of facts and knowledge, but also as the questioning of actions and behaviour in ways that improve performance.

One of the lessons from the changeover process in which Stayer engaged was the realization that he could not wait until he had a clear picture of how the new systems would work to make the changes – he had to learn his way through the process.

He explains that the process was not neat and orderly. 'There were lots of obstacles and challenges, much backsliding, and myriad false starts and wrong decisions' (Stayer, 1990, p. 79). For example, when teams were created and chose their team leaders, almost immediately those leaders began to act like supervisors – they fell into the familiar roles. Stayer discovered that they needed training in order to act differently.

Structural changes were made as well. As teams took over many of the processes, less management was needed. The hierarchy went from six layers to three. Staff positions were eliminated when teams took on the selection, training and evaluating roles. Supervisor jobs disappeared when teams took on operational functions of schedules, performance standards, assignments, budgets and capital improvements. The quality control function changed its focus and became technical support to production people.

One example of the information/responsibility pairing is the decision Johnsonville faced in 1985 about whether to accept an offer from a food-processing company to buy large quantities of product on a regular basis. Johnsonville did not have the capacity to handle the job. Before the changeover, Stayer would have gathered his management team and they would have hammered out the pros and cons and made a strategic decision. What Stayer did in this situation was to call a meeting of the whole organization, giving them all of the information he had and asking them to work in teams to answer three questions: What will it take to make it work? Is it possible to reduce the downside? Do we want to do it? The teams struggled with the questions for almost two weeks, wrestling with the risks, which were considerable, and how they would have to operate to accomplish that much increase in production. In the end the teams almost unanimously decided to take on the new business.

Outcomes

From 1982 to 1990 Johnsonville's return on assets has doubled, sales have increased eight-fold and rejects have been reduced from 5 per cent to less than 0.5 per cent. Since 1982, productivity has increased nearly 300 per cent. Johnsonville Foods is in 45 states with sales of $150 million, 600 employees, and three manufacturing facilities. Some of this improvement should be credited to improved technology, but Johnsonville Food's leaders believe the learning initiative is largely responsible. Stayer says, 'If you issue orders, you're telling people, Don't think; just do. But if you've got 1000 people, you've got 1000 minds. And if you issue orders from the top, you're using only 3 of them, or 2, or one. That's stupid' (Brokaw and Hartman, 1990, p. 50).

Figure 4.5 places the learning processes of Johnsonville Foods in the organizational learning cycle. Of the three cases, Johnsonville Foods is the only one in which a change effort was made; the other two examples had the luxury of selecting personnel

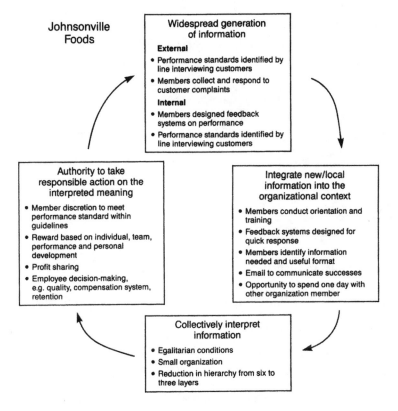

Figure 4.5   The organizational learning cycle for Johnsonville Foods

and establishing norms with learning in mind. Stayer has help-fully chronicled some of the change process so we are able to understand what worked and what did not.

In the first step of the organizational learning cycle, wide-spread generation of information, we can see that change played out in the performance standards that did not work until employees themselves got involved by clarifying them with customers. In the second step as well we see the change process: MIS changes from controlling information to a service to members for identifying what information they will need and the form in which it is needed. The third step, collectively interpreting information, as with Chaparral Steel, can be attributed to the size of the organization, which has deliberately been kept small. The process in which the organization engaged to reach the decision to take on the new business is a good example of collective interpretation. From the description it is clear that this decision was not a matter of a vote, but was a thoughtful interpretation of organization-wide data. The fourth step, authority to take responsible action on the interpreted meaning, was Stayer's original goal. His chronicle makes clear the difficulty of accomplishing that unless the other three steps are in place.

References

Brokaw, L. and Hartman, C. (1990). 'Managing the journey'. *Inc*, Nov-ember, 45–54.

Chaparral Steel Apprenticeship Program (1987). Midlothian: Chap-arral Steel.

Honald, L. (1991). 'The power of learning at Johnsonville Foods'. *Training*, April, 55–8.

Kolb, D. A. (1984). *Experiential Learning*. Englewood Cliffs NJ: Prentice-Hall.

Leonard-Barton, D. (1992). 'The factory as a learning laboratory'. *Sloan Management Review*, Fall, 23–38.

Mahler, H. (1975). 'Smallpox – point of no return'. *World Health*, February/March, 3.

Stayer, R. (1990). 'How I learned to let my workers lead'. *Harvard Business Review*, **68** (6), 66–83.

Background reading

Douglas, J. H. (1975). 'Death of a disease'. *Science News*, **107** (February), 74–5. (World Health Organization.)

Dumaine, B. (1992). 'Chaparral Steel: Unleash workers and cut costs'. *Fortune*, **125** (10), 18. (Chaparral Steel.)

Forward, G. E., Beach, D. E., Gray, D. A. and Quick, J. C. (1991). 'Mentofacturing: a vision for American industrial excellence'. *Academy of Management Executive*, **5** (3), 32–44. (Chaparral Steel.)

Henderson, D. A. (1976). 'The eradication of smallpox'. *Scientific American*, **235** (4), 25–33. (World Health Organization.)

Henderson, D. A. (1977). 'Smallpox shows the way'. February/March, 22–7. (World Health Organization.)

Hopkins, J. W. (1988). 'The eradication of smallpox: Organizational learning and innovation in international health administration'. *The Journal of Developing Areas*, **22**, 321–32. (World Health Organization.)

Kantrow, A. M. (1986). 'Wide-open management at Chaparral Steel'. *Harvard Business Review*, **64** (3), 96–102. (Chaparral Steel.)

Lee, C. (1990). 'Beyond teamwork'. *Training*, **2** (6), 25–32. (Johnsonville Foods.)

Luthans, F. (1991). 'Conversation with Gordon Forward'. *Organizational Dynamics*, **20** (1), 63–72. (Chaparral Steel.)

McKague, A. (1992). 'Learning culture vital'. *Computing Canada*, **18** (3), 11. (Chaparral Steel.)

McManus, G. J. (1992). 'Beaming with pride'. *Iron Age*, 14–17. (Chaparral Steel.)

Quick, J. C. and Gray, D. A. (1989/90). 'Chaparral Steel Company: Bringing "world class manufacturing" to steel'. *National Productivity Review*, **9** (1), 51–8. (Chaparral Steel.)

5 A theoretical framework for organizational learning

In this chapter I want to add much greater detail to each step of the organizational learning cycle. I have extrapolated some of the elements that are critical from the three case studies and have added some examples from other organizations as well in an attempt to round out the description. I have also provided supporting theory where it is available. Although much less theoretical and empirical research has been done on collective learning than individual learning, there are some findings that can add depth to the anecdotal information provided in the case studies. Figure 5.1 displays the abstracted elements related to each step of the organizational learning cycle.

Step 1 – Widespread generation of information

I have used the term 'generate' for this step of the organizational learning cycle to encompass both the collection of external data and the internal development of new ideas, including both process and product. Within external information I include

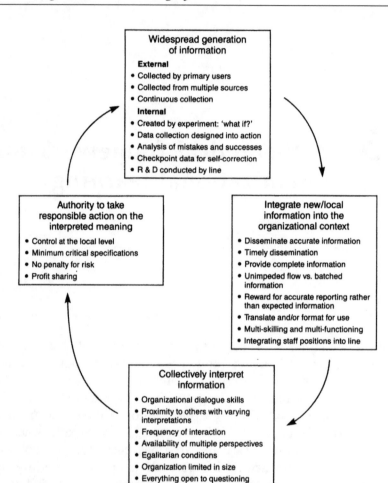

Figure 5.1   Elements in the organizational learning cycle

information about customers, suppliers, new technology and
economic conditions, to name a few of many possible sources
of information. Generating external information requires
crossing the organization's boundaries to interact with the
world external to the organization. By contrast, internal information is developed through the process of conducting the
organization's business and occurs within the boundaries of
the organization. It includes analysing successes and mistakes,

creating experiments designed to provide new information, and building checkpoints into activities so that the activity can become self correcting.

There is a second operative term in the label of this first step: 'widespread'. I am suggesting that the generation of information needs to be the responsibility of all members of the organization rather than leaving those tasks to specialized functions, such as R&D or customer service.

External information

The rationale for shared responsibility was, to some extent, explained in Chapter 2 in discussing the importance of differences for learning. It is not difference itself but the resolution of differences through self-confrontation that is at the heart of learning.

For individual learning, self-confrontation means an individual is able to hold multiple views in his or her mind at one time in order to make sense of them. For organizational learning, self-confrontation means that an individual, as a subsystem of the organization, must be able to confront others who have constructed a different meaning. Likewise, one department must be able to confront another department which has constructed a meaning unique to it. Friedlander (1983) says, 'Organizational learning occurs at the interfaces between persons, between organizational units, and between the organization and its external environment' (p. 199). As each subsystem interacts with the external environment and then internally with other subsystems it creates a unique perspective which it then adds to the diversity of ideas and to the diversity of relationships that can be built among those ideas. Diversity of ideas and perspectives is necessary for learning through self-confrontation to occur. We have many societal examples of disparate ideas leading to new learning: the difficulties between sexes have caused a new and more equitable way of being, the difficulties between Japan and the US has led to improved quality, and the differences between handicapped and non-handicapped has led to a more humane society. Difference, as uncomfortable as it often makes us, leads to learning.

Useful difference within an organization is created when individual members experience the environment in which they function first-hand, rather than through the organized information provided by others. Because all information is influenced and shaped by those who collect it, information that is collected centrally and then distributed has already gone through several layers of filters, which have shaped and to some extent homogenized it.

A basic tenet of systems theory is that heterogeneity produces energy whereas complete homogeneity leads to entropy. A closed system will increasingly develop a homogeneous view; the accessible meaning structures of organizational members will gradually become collective meaning structures and disappear from the organizational dialogue. Diversity is created by opening the organizational boundaries to let in new views.

I am not, however, suggesting a massive duplicative effort where everyone collects every kind of information the organization needs; rather, I am suggesting that information be collected by the primary users of the data. By primary users I mean those who will act on the information. The example of the line workers at Johnsonville Foods directly receiving complaint letters from customers is an illustration of primary users collecting information. There are other unique ways organizations have of involving primary users in the collection of external data. For example, an innovative hospital pays its employees to visit hospitals in other parts of the country while they are on vacation. In these visits what the employee attends to most closely is the function he or she performs back home.

Diversity of meaning is also encouraged by collecting data from multiple sources. Many organizations limit their data collection to standard practices, such as focus groups or customer surveys, but as all three case examples illustrate the informal sources are often as productive as the formal. For example, one construction firm asks employees to note any new construction sites they see on their way to and from work. Another company has a 'competitor alert' file to which managers all contribute on a regular basis. Price-Waterhouse uses a computer program to scan news for any articles on customers. The articles are automatically sent to the partners who are working with those customers.

A final factor related to external information in Figure 5.1 is continuous collection. The external collection of information is not just to seek a specific answer to an identified problem but serves to identify and raise problems as well. For example, the teams at Chaparral that network to gain access to new technology are looking for opportunity as much as answers – a continuous process.

The continuous collection of information by primary users and through multiple sources is only workable if the second step of the organizational learning cycle is in place. Information about the external environment cannot be closely held but must be made available to others; it must become a part of the organizational context. However, before turning to the second step of the organizational learning cycle it is important to focus on the development of internal information.

Internal generation of information

Organizational members in all three of the case examples were heavily involved in generating new information. The factory workers at Chaparral thought of the factory floor as a learning laboratory and designed experiments as a part of carrying out their jobs. The fieldworkers of WHO thought of themselves as researchers. Some experiments are like pilot projects conducted in order to find out if a certain process will work well enough to warrant implementing it more widely. Other experiments are initiated for the purpose of gaining information that will inform related decisions. When Chaparral decided to go with the 24-inch product because it was more 'technically challenging' their purpose was to learn something from the experience that might help them in other areas. They were designing their work in ways that generated information as well as got the job done. 'In any design process questions arise for which objective answers are not available . . . they must be dealt with by incorporation into the design experimental processes for resolving them' (Ackoff, 1981, p. 106).

3M, an organization considered a world-class leader in

innovation, reportedly encourages experimentation by allocating 10 per cent of employees' time to working on their own experiments. The example of the maintenance workers who developed a machine to strap bundles of steel rods reflects Chaparral's attitude towards experimenting with new solutions.

When we think about learning from our actions we often mean taking time to reflect at the end of a project or event to consider whether it was a success or failure. That can be a valuable process to help us learn from our actions. We can think of these end-of-project post-mortems as summative evaluation, a kind of report card. There is another type of evaluation, formative, whose purpose is not judgement but course correction. This kind of evaluation happens not at the end of an initiative but during. The analogue might be a self-guided missile which continually takes readings and uses them to correct its course. In one computer manufacturing company, each team starts the morning with a 15-minute meeting to review its performance results from the day before. If the results were poor the team works on solving the problem. If the results were good they think through ways to keep the curve moving upward. Revans (1983) has noted: 'Any system that is to learn . . . must regularly receive and interpret inputs about its own outputs' (p. 13). But to accomplish formative evaluation, the plan for data collection must be established up-front. The question consistently asked by organizational members in the three case examples is not only 'What can we do?' but 'What can we learn from what we do?'.

Step 2 – Integrating new/local information into the organizational context

Information that is collected externally and/or generated internally can only be understood within the context of the total organization. The silo phenomenon in organizations is when one part of the organization does not have access to what other parts know (in effect, it cannot learn from them), and it is often decried for this reason. But an equally detrimental effect of the silo phenomenon is the inability of each part to understand its own information because it lacks the context of the whole picture. It would be like closely examining a single piece of a jigsaw puzzle without access to the other pieces. The billing people at Chaparral benefit from the multi-functioning described, not only because they are better able to answer related questions such as those about shipping, but because in knowing about shipping they are better able to answer billing questions.

In order to accomplish the organization's task we must act in concert with each other, and to do that we must share some understanding about what we are trying to accomplish and how we are going about it. Schon (1979) provides an example of shared understanding in his description of a simple craft organization. He first describes the activities of an individual craftsman who is not part of an organization and therefore does all of the many tasks involved in making wooden shovels himself – from selecting logs from which to shape the shovels, to pricing the end product in order to make a profit. Schon suggests that the craftsman carries a picture in his head of the total task and of the relationship of each sub-task to the whole. When the making of shovels is accomplished by a small group of individuals, an organization, instead of a single individual, the sub-tasks are divided among them – but the individuals must still maintain in their heads an image of the whole and the relationship of their parts to it in order to insure that their sub-tasks will fit the whole. For example, the worker who rough cuts the shovels needs to hold an image similar to the one that the worker who fine chisels the shovels holds and so on. Schon explains that 'whereas the individual craftsman controlled the pattern of his own activities, control in the workshop is partly an individual and partly a collective matter' (p. 117).

The distribution of accurate and complete information is a critical element in the integration of new or local information into the organizational context, yet the type and amount of information that is disseminated within organizations is often limited. There are four methods through which the distribution of information is obstructed: message routing, message summarizing, message delay, and message modification (Daft and Huber, 1987). Message routing is the selective distribution of information. Message summarizing is the reduction of the size of the message, for example, reducing large sets of numbers to averages. Message delay relates to when the message is distributed. Message modification is the distortion of meaning. These four methods affect the availability, form and accuracy of information in the organization.

These methods are often used by upper management to control the information employees receive, but they are as frequently used by employees to control the information upper management receives. They are also used to negative effect between sub-units. Examples of such control might include:

- employees modifying negative information that is being reported upward so that it will reflect less negatively on the sender
- management delaying a message to employees until a more favourable time
- a manufacturing department benchmarking a product but giving little thought as to who else in the organization could benefit from the benchmark information
- the organization purchasing an environmental scan for the use of the planning team, but not disseminating the information beyond the level of upper management.

The use of message routing, summarizing, delay and modification to control information may be deliberate on the part of any segment of the organization, but such processes are equally likely to be a part of the collective meaning structure of the organization: 'simply the way we do things around here'. Therefore, to resolve the problems related to the distribution of information, the organization must not only create better processes for distribution, it must also question the collective meaning structure that mediates the full and accurate distribution of information.

The elements needed for the second step of the organizational learning cycle are the converse of message routing, summarizing, delay, and modification. All parts of the organization need to provide all other parts with accurate, timely and complete information. The WHO case example illustrates the importance of information: without the courageous choice to report accurate rather than politically sensitive information, the smallpox campaign would have failed. Another example of the dissemination of complete information is the Kao Corporation, where all company information (excepting personnel data) is stored in a single integrated database that is open to any employee regardless of position.

Timeliness of information is illustrated by the Chaparral's metaphor of the unimpeded flow of information rather than batched information. General Electric Aircraft Engines is developing an organization-wide project planning system to both design and store the many projects through which its business is run. This process will integrate the information from projects across the entire system. The consistency in format and documentation will provide the capability to retrieve individual projects or classes of projects which are related by some salient factor.

The case example of the WHO also demonstrates the need for rewarding accurate reporting. The level and quality of local outbreak reports increased when a mobile surveillance team provided personal contact. It is difficult for any of us to send reports down what often seems to be a black hole. Even disseminating information is, to some extent, an interactive process: we need some sense of how our report was received and to what use it was put. In one organization, run largely on a project basis, a brief description of each project is put on the organization's electronic bulletin board. Following the description an impact list is provided, that is, a list of other projects or functional areas that the project members believe will be affected in some way by the project. The description is automatically sent to those on the list, as are weekly updates on the progress of the projects. Frequent response and inquiries from those on the impact list encourage the senders to persist and help them understand more clearly the level of detail that others need as well as the ways in which the information is being put to use.

Tushman and Scanlan (1981) note that specialization within organizations may interfere with information distribution. Specialization increases the efficiency of information processing within a unit, but is a double-edged sword in that it often blocks information from moving across unit boundaries. Idiosyncratic language and local conceptual frameworks work against the distribution of information across specializations. Thus the need for boundary-spanning individuals who are able to understand and translate the information and facilitate shared under-standing across organization boundaries. In one highly technical organization, a position of translator or interpreter has been created to bridge the gap between specialisms (materials, design, finance). These boundary-spanning professionals work in the 'cracks' of the organization, translating what one specialism is doing for the benefit of another. In a very different sense, Springfield Remanufacturing Corporation also engages in a kind of translation. It uses a continuous scrolling display on the shop floor to display the organization's performance on numerous indicators. To make sure the indicators have meaning to the viewers, everyone is trained in how to read financial information.

Organizations have found unique ways of integrating infor-mation, for example, Johnsonville Foods' policy of giving each employee one day a year to spend with an employee in another department. At Toyota Canada, departments invite employees from other departments into their monthly meetings. They also take staff on tours of the company. Honda requires each manager to exchange jobs for a two-week period with a counter-part in another function. At some General Motors plants performance evaluations include an item on networking that encourages the integration of information. GE has implemented a best practices seminar in which internal best practices are explained in detail and teams from other units have time to plan together about how they might implement the practice in their own unit. In a similar vein, NASA has regularly scheduled success sharing meetings, the purpose of which is to inform others of projects or events that have 'gone right'.

Chaparral Steel provides helpful examples of using multi-functioning and multi-skilling to integrate information, such as the factory workers who have business cards for when they act as sales representatives, the fork-lift operators who do their own routine maintenance, and the janitors who enter customer orders into the system. At both Chaparral Steel and Johnsonville Foods many of the staff functions have been integrated into line responsibilities. At Johnsonville, for example, staff hire, measure employee performance and make disciplinary contracts when necessary.

Step 3 – Collectively interpreting the information

Of paramount importance to organizational learning are the processes that are in place to facilitate organizational members collectively interpreting information, the third step of the organizational learning cycle. It is easy to make the mistake of equating giving others information with learning. Leaders often think that if they have widely distributed information, organizational members will 'know it'. As we saw in Chapter 2, receiving information and making meaning from it are very different processes. When an individual is given information, he or she selectively attends to it. Those parts which are selected are examined for patterns and are compared to the meaning the individual has stored in long-term memory. Only when the individual has formed new relationships through this process and again stored those new relationships in long-term memory can we say the individual has learned.

For organizational learning to occur the process is yet more complex. Not only must each individual engage in the sequence just described, each must do so while interacting with other organizational members (who are of course engaged in the same sequence themselves) and out of their interaction the organizational members must form an interpretation of the information.

I want to stop short of saying that they must agree upon an interpretation. The goal of collective interpretation is more the reduction in the equivocality of information than reaching consensus. By engaging in collective interpretation each person involved is influenced by the meanings others hold and in turn influences the meanings of others. Each better understands the reasoning and data others are using to arrive at their meaning; thus they understand others' meanings more fully and by comparison, understand their own more fully. Collective interpretation may not develop a definitive answer, but if organizational members fully invest themselves in collective interpretation, they will understand the parameters of the problem more clearly.

The difficult question Johnsonville Foods faced, related to whether to take on the additional work that would stretch its production capacity, is perhaps a useful illustration. There was no textbook answer to the three questions Stayer put to the members of the organization, and even when all the available data pertaining to the issue were laid out, clear-cut answers were still not obvious. It was only through the many days of wrestling with the information that the equivocality was reduced and an interpretation was reached upon which the group agreed to act. Even so, the report was that it was nearly unanimous, not that it was unanimous. We do not all have to be in total agreement in order to act in concert. We do, however, all need to understand fully the reasoning behind the proposed action, and moreover we need the opportunity to influence that reasoning. Collective interpretation provides both opportunities.

In the Johnsonville Foods example the collective interpretation occurred through a relative, formal set of meetings. At Chaparral Steel collective interpretation often occurs spontaneously with a group coming together on the factory floor to deal with a problem that has just arisen. The level of formality is less critical than are the conditions that allow collective interpretation to occur.

However, before turning to those conditions, I want to contrast collective interpretation of information with the more traditional way organizations have attempted to interpret widely dispersed knowledge. Traditionally, someone in a management or supervisory position collects relevant information from subordinates and, armed with the collective information, interprets it and arrives at a conclusion. Then, based on this interpretation, the supervisor informs subordinates of the actions to take. This is the approach Stayer describes as the way he would have made the production decision before he began the change process. This funnel approach, in which one individual (or sometimes a team) serves as the conduit for the collective information, may be able to take into account some of the information that each individual has to contribute, but it cannot make use of the reasoning they might contribute – and that is a considerable loss to learning. The funnel model is based on assumptions that are antithetical to organizational learning:

1   That information is an accurate representation of reality that, when summed, can provide a 'right' answer, rather than being an interpretation.
2   That it is the information individuals have rather than their meaning-making capability that is most valuable.
3   That learning is one-way rather than a joint activity in which the meaning structures of both or all parties are modified.

Conditions that enhance collective interpretation of information

We can each name organizations in which we have interacted with our colleagues on a regular basis but where very little collective interpretation occurred. The opportunity to interact is not enough: there must be conditions in place that support collective interpretation. Those conditions include:

* information and expertise that are distributed
* egalitarian values
* the organization's size and physical arrangement support frequent interaction between subsystems
* processes and skills that facilitate organizational dialogue.

Information and expertise that are distributed

Information must be distributed among the individuals engaged in collective interpretation rather than residing in only one or two individuals. If only one or very few organizational members have all of the information related to a subject, collective interpretation is not useful. Step 1 of the organizational learning cycle, in which every individual engages in the collection of external information and in the generation of internal information related to their own function is one way distributed information is achieved. Chaparral sends teams all over the world to look at new technology, talk with competitors and interact with university researchers. These organizational members have first-hand information to bring to organizational interactions.

Having organizational members continually engage in individual training and learning opportunities is a way to achieve distributed expertise. Both Johnsonville Foods and Chaparral Steel place great emphasis on internal training and external educational opportunities. At Chaparral 90 per cent of employees are involved in training, and at Johnsonville 65 per cent – both far exceeding industry averages, particularly for first-line employees.

Egalitarian values

There are three core values that enhance collective interpretation:

- *freedom* to speak openly without fear of punishment or coercion
- *equality*, which must exist for freedom to exist
- *respect*, which must be present for equality to exist.

It should not be surprising that freedom and learning are connected. Thomas Jefferson made it clear that without learning that resulted in informed opinion, freedom could not prevail. The converse is also true: without freedom, learning is limited to what others will permit.

'Equality' means that no individual's ideas are more worthy

(more right) than any other's by virtue of position or status. The meaning that each individual has constructed is tested against the meanings of others, not against the power or position of others.

'Respect' acknowledges that each individual has constructed meaning structures that make 'sense' to him or her. It acknowledges that there is a logic to their construction that, if we could only grasp it, would allow us to share their world. The other side of respect is humility, the realization that the way I have constructed the world is only my interpretation, which is certain to change. Paulo Freire (1970) says:

On the other hand, dialogue cannot exist without humility. The naming of the world, through which people constantly re-create the world, cannot be an act of arrogance. Dialogue, as the encounter of those addressed to the common task of learning and acting, is broken if the parties (or one of them) lack humility. How can I dialogue if I always project ignorance onto others and never perceive my own? How can I dialogue if I regard myself as a case apart from others – mere 'its' in whom I cannot recognize other 'Is'? How can I dialogue if I consider myself a member of the in-group of 'pure' men, the owners of truth and knowledge, for whom all non-members are 'these people' of 'the great unwashed?' . . . How can I dialogue if I am closed to – and even offended by – the contribution of others? How can I dialogue if I am afraid of being displaced, the mere possibility causing me torment and weakness? Self-sufficiency is incompatible with dialogue. People who lack humility (or have lost it) . . . cannot be their partners in naming the world. (p. 78)

To place collective interpretation at the heart of organizational learning is to affirm the power of the individual mind and equally to affirm the power of the collective mind. It is a Jeffersonian concept that acknowledges the capability of individuals to think for themselves, to manage themselves, to govern themselves. It is an affirmation of democratic ideals over autocratic ideals.

Perhaps one of the reasons so little organizational learning occurs is that the conditions of freedom, equality and respect so rarely exist in organizations. Organizations will not be able to learn effectively until these are manifest.

There is some research evidence that egalitarian values lead to greater organizational learning. Brooks (1993) in a study of collective learning in quality teams says, 'The greatest barrier to collective team learning encountered by the teams ... was the assumption that some contributions were more valuable than others' (p. 54). In this study it was not the fact that some members knew more than others that limited learning, but the perception of the worth of others' ideas. Conversely, in studies in which organizational members believed others possessed or could construct answers more easily than themselves, they were less willing to do the hard work of learning (Hatano and Inagaki, 1991). I remember Malcolm Knowles, heralded as the father of adult education, as a white-haired octogenarian, saying that one of the most frustrating problems about getting older was that when he spoke to a group, out of respect no one would challenge his ideas, and thus his own learning was severely inhibited. Such inhibitions may occur because of position, perceived expertise, years of experience or a myriad of other factors that cause individuals to experience an imbalance in the relationship.

Hierarchy is a great inhibitor to learning. Friedlander (1983) says, 'Power differences hinder system learning when subordinate components suppress or deny their own resources and expertise, when superior components impose theirs, or when either party distances itself from the other, for example, in order to protect itself' (p. 200). It is not only lower-level employees who are likely to learn less when those higher in the hierarchy are present; those individuals who are higher in the hierarchy are also less likely to develop new ideas, because their ideas are not challenged (Hatano and Inagaki, 1991).

Since it is not feasible to eliminate organizational hierarchy, at least in the foreseeable future, organizational members must work at establishing rules and norms which reduce or eliminate its negative impact on collective interpretation. Chaparral works at reducing its effects by such things as all employees being salaried, no special parking and no special dining facilities.

Other organizations have developed unique techniques for reducing the learning effects of hierarchy. At Granite Rock, all levels of employee are trained together: there is not the usual segregation by level. At the Corkstown facility of Northern Telecom organizational members have created a 'pink room'. In this room hierarchy does not exist, and colleagues can be forthright in their opinions or ask each other for help with assurance that what is said stays in the pink room.

Size

Collective interpretation is assisted when organizational members have the opportunity for frequent face-to-face interaction. Both Chaparral Steel and Johnsonville Foods have been deliberate about keeping their size small to facilitate that interaction. Although research has not shown how large an organization might be and still be able to engage in collective interpretation of information, it seems obvious that mega-organizations that number in the thousands make many of the conditions listed here unlikely. Chaparral has, as well, designed its building to facilitate interaction. Mars has also used the physical arrangement of its offices to facilitate interaction between levels and departments. The offices are arranged in a pie-shape, with the company officers in the middle. Some organizations use 'caves' and 'coves' to facilitate interaction. Caves are offices only large enough for one person and his or her computer. Coves are common areas with sofas and overstuffed chairs. They have flip charts and coffee available. If organizational members need to meet with others they must do so in the common area where their colleagues are also meeting. Individual offices behind closed doors would seem to represent a time when we thought of work as an individual task. As we think about work as the function of a team and collective interpretation as a necessity, surely the physical environment of our organizations as well as their size will be modified.

Organizational dialogue

Organizational dialogue is interaction in a collective setting that results in mutual learning upon which the organization can act. In defining dialogue in this way I am restricting its use to a specific kind of organizational talk; talk that reveals our meaning structures to each other. When that happens we learn and our partners in dialogue learn as well – we achieve a kind of mutual learning. But that is not a common kind of talk in organizations. I am also reserving the term dialogue for a collective setting: two people engaged in a conversation, although important for collective interpretation, would not be organizational dialogue in the sense I am using it here. It may also be important to address the last phrase in the definition, 'upon which the organization can act'. I am, then, not just talking about good communication skills or making another 'feel' heard or feel better about themselves; rather I am implying interaction that is targeted to the organization's business.

To carry on a dialogue the conditions I have described in this section need to be in place. In addition, participants need the skills to:

- provide others with accurate and complete information that bears upon the issue
- confirm others' personal competence when disagreeing with their ideas
- make the reasoning that supports their position explicit; say how they got from the data to the conclusion
- voice the perspective of others
- change position when others offer convincing data and rationale
- regard assertions, their own and others, as hypotheses to be tested
- challenge errors in others' reasoning or data.

The use of the term 'skills' for this list may be somewhat misleading. The items on this list might, in fact, seem self-evident to most of us; the reader might say, 'Of course we need all of the available information that pertains to the issue we are considering'. Yet as a researcher who has observed meetings in many organizations, I know that the actual use of these behaviours is rare. It is much more frequent, for example, for participants in a discussion to withhold critical information for fear that it might embarrass themselves or others, to offer their conclusions but not the data on which they were based, and to regard their own position as 'truth' and others' positions as in error.

If the skills appear self-evident yet are in little use, we have to wonder whether there is a skill issue or if it is just that the organizational conditions in which most of us function have made the use of these behaviours hazardous. Drawing on the theory of individual learning described in Chapter 2, I would suggest that we have made not these skills, but their converse, tacit. We have so often withheld our reasoning, refrained from saying what we know others do not want to hear, and held on to our position long after the evidence has proved us wrong, that it is those behaviours that have become automatic. That implies that if we want to employ these skills of dialogue, we may first have to 'unlearn' the tacit ones that are preventing effective dialogue.

In constructing this list of skills for dialogue I have drawn upon the work of several theorists who have written extensively about dialogue: Argyris, Bohm, Mezirow, and Johnson and Johnson.

Provide others with accurate and complete information that bears upon the issue

The operative phrase in this statement is 'that bears upon the issue'. It is not an argument for total honesty or for saying anything that is on our minds, but rather it speaks to an implicit obligation to a group struggling with an issue to put all relevant information, the good and the bad, on the table so that we all have the information.

Our tendency, however, is to withhold that part of the information that we believe will make us look bad or that we fear will embarrass someone else. Rather than risk that embarrassment we often try to persuade others using substitute arguments and in so doing we add to the equivocality and make the collective interpretation more difficult. Perhaps most importantly we prevent others from correcting us if the information we are so closely guarding is mistaken.

There is a kind of arrogance about withholding the information that we fear will embarrass others. It implies, 'I know what is best for you', removing from others the responsibility for their own actions. Likewise, there is a prejudice suggested in withholding information that we fear will make ourselves look bad. It implies that others will be intolerant of our error, without offering them the opportunity to behave in a tolerant manner. It prejudges others and again prevents us from finding out if we are wrong.

Challenge the errors in others' reasoning or data

The polite response to hearing what we know to be a mistake in a colleague's reasoning or errors in their facts is to not mention it and to change the subject. Our good intention is to 'save face'. It is, however, the uncertainty provoked by such a challenge which leads to the reorganization of one's meaning structures. Johnson and Johnson (1989) describe what happens when we challenge another's ideas:

1   When individuals are presented with a problem or decision, they have an initial conclusion based on categorizing and organizing incomplete information, their limited experiences, and their specific perspective.
2   When individuals present their conclusion and its rationale to others, they engage in cognitive rehearsal, deepening their understanding of their position, and discover higher-level reasoning strategies.
3   Individuals are confronted by other people with different conclusions based on other people's information, experiences, and perspectives.
4   Individuals become uncertain as to the correctness of their

views. A state of conceptual conflict or disequilibrium is aroused.

5 Uncertainty, conceptual conflict, and disequilibrium motivates an active search for more information, new experiences, and a more adequate cognitive perspective and reasoning process in hopes of resolving the uncertainty . . .

6 By adapting their cognitive perspective and reasoning through understanding and accommodating the perspective and reasoning of others, a new reconceptualized, and reorganized conclusion is derived. Novel solutions and decisions that, on balance, are qualitatively better are detected (pp. 91–2).

When we forgo challenging others, we reduce their learning and ours.

Confirm others' personal competence when disagreeing with their ideas

When we challenge a colleague's reasoning or data we hope they will respond with insight and appreciation. It is sometimes the case that even with our repeated attempts to 'make them understand' our colleague does not change his or her view. We are then likely to experience dissonance ourselves. How is it that our colleague could fail to see what is so obvious to us? We find ourselves with only two ways we can get ourselves out of the dilemma we have created, neither of which is comfortable. We can reconsider whether our own view might be wrong, or we can assume that our colleague is just not smart (open, experienced, honest) enough to see what is so obvious to us. It is the latter choice that causes us to attack our colleague's competence, although we often do it with the subtleness of language and tone. This dichotomous thinking into which we place ourselves leaves us needing to place blame, or wrongness, on one side or the other. One way out of this dilemma is perspective taking.

Voice the perspective of others

Voicing perspective is the act of paraphrasing the ideas and arguments of others. Perspective taking is more than just being able to play back others' arguments in order to check with them for accuracy. It is the ability to comprehend and voice how the situation appears from another's perspective. Perspective taking is the opposite of egocentrism, in which the individual is locked into a single view of the situation and is unaware of the limitations of that view or that other viable perspectives may exist.

When one voices the perspective of another, that action inclines the other to disclose information more fully than if the perspective was not voiced. The additional information and the fuller comprehension of another perspective both work to increase the development of new knowledge out of varying perspectives on a complex issue. However, it is necessary to hold both one's own and others' perspectives in mind at the same time to develop new knowledge. Simply listening to another's perspective is less facilitative of the creation of new knowledge than is the actual voicing of the other's perspective. We place such a high value on information that it is almost counter-intuitive to realize that the amount of actual information within a group is less important in reaching a high-quality solution to a problem than is voicing others' perspectives.

Make the reasoning that supports one's own position explicit

We are inclined to be parsimonious in our talk. We do not want to bore others or be accused of saying to them what they already know. So we often talk in shorthand; we state our conclusions but not our data. We speak at a high level of abstraction and leave out the examples that would illustrate our meaning. We make declarative statements in a way that indicates to others that the statements are self-evident; we say 'That just will not work!'. Ambrose Bierce defined 'self-evident' as evident to oneself and to nobody else.

But, as we saw in Chapter 2, each of us makes very different interpretations of the information we receive. We construct very different meanings for terms like honesty, integrity, empowerment and responsibility. To make our meaning clear to others or to make use of others to correct our meaning, we have to offer our reasoning as well as our conclusions. We have to say not only what we think, but why we think that. In so doing we give others the opportunity to determine for themselves whether the data warrants the conclusion.

Although the cognitive benefits to the receiver of such an exchange are apparent, there is evidence that it is the speaker who makes the greatest cognitive gains from such an exchange. Recent studies have shown that the act of orally summarizing information works to strengthen the speaker's understanding of that information. Such a finding would seem to bear out the insight of the Roman philosopher who said '*Qui docet descit*'. Whoever teaches learns twice. Individuals organize information differently if they are going to present it to others than if they are trying to understand it for their own sake. It is in the act of speaking that we tend to organize cognitively what we know.

Change position when others offer convincing data and rationale

This skill is about being willing to be influenced by the cogent arguments of others: using logical reasoning to determine when the conclusions of others are valid. We sometimes think of changing positions in pejorative terms as 'giving in'. But this skill is not about losing or compromising, it is about making an agreement with others that we will use the capability of our minds to make sense of the information. We will not say something makes sense when it does not, and we will change our position when the data are convincing.

Regard assertions, our own and others', as hypotheses to be tested

This is probably the most difficult of all the skills to implement. It is not so difficult for us to hold others' assertions as hypotheses to be tested, but incredibly difficult for us to hold our own. The way Argyris (1986) suggests that we deal with this difficulty is to ask others for help; that we literally end our statement or conclusion with a request for others to tell us if they see it differently; to ask others to help us see where we may be mistaken.

Bohm (1985) says simply, ideas must be vulnerable. 'We have to have enough faith in our world-view to work from it, but not that much faith that we think it's the final answer' (p. 4).

It is difficult to use the skills I have listed here in the fast-paced, business as usual, environment of most organizations. To have organizational dialogue it is necessary to establish the time needed. That time does not, of course, need to be time away from work, because the dialogue is about the work. The meetings that Johnsonville Foods had to think through the production capacity were a time set aside for dialogue. There are other ways to deal with the time issue. In some meetings there is an identified time for dialogue and a separate time for discussion.

Changing tacit organizational assumptions

A paradox of organizational learning is that organizations can only learn through their individual members, yet organizations create systemic constraints that prevent their individual members from learning.

Argyris (1990) suggests some familiar organizational practices that limit learning, such as transferring poor employees from one division to another rather than firing them; implementing a programme that the implementors know will not solve the problem; softening bad news that is sent upward; concealing an unattractive programme within an attractive one; selling a programme modestly while concealing its magnitude; and getting the agreement of principal players before a meeting while acting in the meeting as though no such agreement has been reached. These organizational practices are not written down but may, nevertheless, be understood by organizational members as the way to get things done in this organization. They can be explained as organizational theories of action; if you want to accomplish A under circumstances B then do C (see Figure 5.2). To use one of the examples listed above, if (A) you want to get management support for a programme when

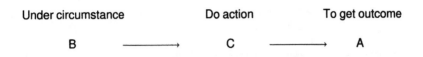

Figure 5.2   Argyris' framework for a theory of action

(B) you believe support will not be forthcoming, then (C) play down the extent of the programme until it has gained a foothold and then ask for what was really needed.

Defensive routines occur because organizational members feel caught. They want to accomplish certain goals assigned to them by the organization; they have learned that the espoused organizational processes will not allow them to accomplish those goals; they believe that they cannot openly address the fact that the espoused processes do not work without embarrassment or threat; they develop a way to accomplish the goals while by-passing the threat; and they develop ways to hide the fact that they have by-passed the threat. Defensive routines become so familiar to organizational members that they become tacit. They are the accepted practice of the organization and have become a part of the collective meaning structures.

There are, however, unintended consequences from such organizational defensive routines. For example, when poorly performing employees are transferred instead of fired, the organization retains a workforce that is inefficient, lowering its productivity and performance. A second and equally serious unintended consequence is that learning is prevented. By circumventing problems, organizational members leave the problem unaddressed. The organization does not learn how to deal with its poor performers because the issue is not openly addressed. Argyris (1990) notes:

Organizational defensive routines are actions or policies that prevent individuals or segments of the organization from experiencing embarrassment or threat. Simultaneously, they prevent people from identifying and getting rid of the causes of the potential embarrassment or threat. Organizational defensive routines are antilearning, overprotective, and self-sealing. (p. 25)

Conditions	Dilemmas and assumptions	Actions	Consequences
Demands and constraints	How organization's members feel caught or what they believe	What organization's members do	Impact on business results, attitudes, relationships

Figure 5.3   Framework for an organizational causal map

Argyris (1986) suggests that to overcome these defensive routines groups of organizational members should work together to map the causal relationships between organizational goals, actions and outcomes, including the unintended consequences (see Figure 5.3). These maps can serve as a vehicle for organizational dialogue about the organization's assumptions. Organizational learning does not occur in the making of the map; the learning is the inquiry which alters these maps in ways that bring the organization's action closer to its espoused theory or perhaps changes both to gain the congruence needed. This public map-making process serves to place the tacit collective meaning structures back into the accessible meaning of the individuals, where it can be challenged, tested and altered.

The maps demonstrate the systemic nature of organizational problems (see Figures 5.4 and 5.5). It is often clear from such maps that the cause is not, for example, managers who are acting improperly, but rather that the system prevents managers from acting in ways that the system wishes managers to act. The solution must also be at the system level.

Collective interpretation of information only works if all individuals actively work towards the learning of others as well as themselves. I am not simply implying a situation in which I will learn what I need from the collective and you must make sure you learn what you need as well. I am suggesting that unless others learn, our own learning is lessened. And moreover, I am suggesting that we have a responsibility to work actively towards the learning of others. Like good tennis players who only improve if their competitors are skilled, my thinking

Conditions	Dilemmas and assumptions	Actions	Consequences
Low productivity	Managers who discipline poor performers are viewed as 'not people-oriented'	When employees perform poorly managers transfer employees to other departments	Large numbers of poor performers are retained in the organization
Organization attempting to improve morale by being more people-oriented	Manager's chances of promotion theatened		The organization does not learn how to deal with poor performers
Strong pressure to reach performance targets		Managers act as if they are following correct organization procedures	

Figure 5.4   Organizational causal map – low productivity

Conditions	Dilemmas and assumptions	Actions	Consequences
Pressure to keep costs low	Distrust of management's ability to understand the needs of the unit	Prepare initial programme request in a way that camouflages the true costs	Management view programme managers as poor judges of cost
Pressure to provide new services			Management tightens budget controls
		Ask for adequate funds after organization is committed to the programme	No learning about how to budget appropriately

Figure 5.5   Organizational causal map – budget

is not sufficiently challenged by someone who cannot apprehend the concept I am considering, or someone who knows so little about my world that I soon tire of the long explanation in preface to the issue I wish to discuss.

Knowledge is one of the few commodities in the world that grows through use. It is not a competition; the more you know the more I can know. If I want to know more I will have to see to it that you know more. That is perhaps, not an easy concept to grasp, schooled as we all were in individual learning, where helping your neighbour learn was called cheating. But that model was from a time in which we thought learning was about taking in a prescribed knowledge, not about 'naming the world'. In organizations we are a community of learners.

Step 4 – Authority to take responsible action based on the interpreted meaning

There is an apocryphal story told about the composer Brahms. He was in a sitting room where someone else was at the piano, idly playing notes and chords. In the middle of playing the pianist abruptly left. After a few moments Brahms got up, went to the piano, and finished the progression. His comment was, 'We cannot let that chord go unresolved forever'. There is, in all of us, a propensity to do what needs doing. That inclination is particularly strong when we are knowledgeable about the issues involved. Brahms's need to resolve the chord progression was acute because he so thoroughly understood what chord should come next in the progression. It was knowledge that pulled him from his chair and into action.

When an organization involves its members in the generation of information and positions that information in the organizational context, and when members collectively interpret that information, but the organization stops short of authorizing organizational members to act on the knowledge they have derived, the learning is lost. To understand what needs doing, but to be prevented from acting on that knowledge leads to anger or despair, or in some situations, subversion.

So strong is the compulsion to act on what we know that in many situations we find organizational members going to great lengths to do what they know needs doing, in spite of clear instructions to the contrary.

That is not to say that organizational members always do what needs to be done. They obviously do not. The circumstance I am referencing relates to action taken when knowledge is also present; that is, organizational members have the necessary information and have come to understand it in their own context. That circumstance is quite different from when someone in authority says 'you should take a certain action' or that 'it is your responsibility to do something', without the organizational member necessarily having knowledge that lends meaning to that action. Under such circumstances it is often quite difficult to get organizational members to take action. In fact, we have a term specifically for that situation: resistance to change.

There were many examples of control at the local level in the three case examples. The fieldworkers with WHO were able to change their procedures to take advantage of local customs. The factory workers at Chaparral not only spontaneously met on the floor to interpret the information collectively, they also had authority to act on their interpretation.

If organizational members are to act responsibly, then they must have enough discretion in their actions to make changes when and where they are needed. Herbst (1974) describes 'minimum critical specification' as specifying 'no more than is absolutely necessary for a system to begin operation so that the system can find its own design' (Morgan and Ramirez, 1983, p. 6). Rather than pre-designing as much as possible, the goal is to pre-design as little as possible. It may, in fact, be necessary to specify only the negatives; that is, the limits of action to be avoided rather than the specific actions to be taken. The story about the development of the Honda City car is that Honda gave the designers only two instructions, 'come up with a product concept fundamentally different from anything the company had ever done before, and second, to make a car that was inexpensive but not cheap' (Nonaka, 1991, p. 100). Gore reportedly takes minimum critical specifications so far as to tell new employees to 'go find yourself a job and come back in 60 days'.

The reduction of risk is as necessary to taking responsible action as is having the authority. Chaparral has a no-risk policy. At Wexner, 'buyers are graded not only on their successes, but also on their failures. Too many hits means the buyer isn't taking enough chances' (*Forbes*, 1987).

Finally, in regard to taking responsible action it is important to note the need for a more equitable way to share in the financial gain of the organization. Both Chaparral and Johnsonville Foods have profit-sharing plans. When organizational members have full information about the organization's profit and loss, when they are apprised of the amount of dollar savings their actions have caused, or the increase in earnings their team's new process has made, when they are asked to be responsible for these actions, they will eventually expect to have an equitable share of the rewards.

I have in this chapter outlined some of the processes and elements organizations have employed to implement each step of the organizational learning cycle. I do not have any sense that I have captured them all nor that the ones I have provided would work well in other organizations. The essence of organizational learning is the organization's ability to use the amazing mental capability of all of its members to create the kind of processes that will improve its own learning capacity.

References

Ackoff, R. L. (1981). *Creating the Corporate Future*. New York: John Wiley & Sons.

Argyris, C. (1986). 'Skilled incompetence'. *Harvard Business Review*, September/October, 74–79.

Argyris, C. (1990). *Overcoming Organizational Defenses*. Boston: Allyn and Bacon.

Bohm, D. (1985). *Unfolding Meaning*. New York: Routledge & Kegan Paul Inc.

Bohm, D. (1990). 'On Dialogue' (transcript). Ojai CA: David Bohm Seminars.

Brooks, A. (1993). 'Collective team learning in work organizations'. *HRD Professors' Network 1993 Conference Proceedings*, Atlanta, Georgia.

Daft, R. L. and Huber, G. P. (1987). 'How organizations learn: A communication framework'. *Research in the Sociology of Organizations*, **5**, 1–36.

Forbes Magazine, (1987), April, p. 26.

Freire, P. (1970). *Pedagogy of the Oppressed*. Harmondsworth: Penguin.

Friedlander, F. (1983). 'Patterns of individual and organizational learning', in S. Srivastva (ed.), *The Executive Mind*, pp. 192–220. San Francisco: Jossey-Bass.

Hatano, G. and Inagaki, K. (1991). 'Sharing cognition through collective comprehension activity', in L. B. Resnick, J. M. Levine, and S. D. Teasley (eds), *Socially Shared Cognition* pp. 331–48. Washington DC: American Psychological Association.

Herbst, P. G. (1974). *Socio-technical Design*. London: Tavistock.

Johnson, D. W. and Johnson, R. T. (1989). *Cooperation and Competition: Theory and Research*. Edina MN: Interaction Book Company.

Mezirow, J. (1991). *Transformative Dimensions of Adult Learning*. San Francisco: Jossey-Bass.

Morgan, G. and Ramirez, R. (1983). 'Action learning: A holographic metaphor for guiding social change'. *Human Relations*, **37** (1), 1–28.

Nonaka, I. (1991). 'The knowledge-creating company'. *Harvard Business Review*, November/December, 96–104.

Revans, R. (1983). *ABC of Action Learning*. London: Chartwell-Bratt.

Schon, D. A. (1979). 'Organizational learning', in G. Morgan (ed.), *Beyond Method: Strategies for Social Research*, pp. 114–127. Newbury Park CA: Sage.

Tushman, M. L., and Scanlan, T. J. (1981). 'Boundary spanning individuals: Their role in information transfer and their antecedents'. *Academy of Management Journal*, **24** (2), 289–305.

6 Infrastructure for organizational learning*

In Chapters 4 and 5 I have outlined a theory about how a collective learns. The theory was displayed in a cycle made up of four steps:

1 Widespread generation of information.
2 Integrating new/local information into the organizational context.
3 Collectively interpreting the information.
4 Authority to take responsible action based on the interpreted meaning.

I discussed why each of these steps was necessary for collective learning and gave some examples of the way several organizations have been involved in each of the steps.

Now, with the help of my colleague, Rick Ross, I want to address the more practical question of how to design an infrastructure that supports the organizational learning cycle. We are using the term infrastructure here in much the way you would

* This chapter is co-authored by Nancy M. Dixon and Rick Ross

125

talk about the infrastructure of a city, that is, the roads, bridges, water systems, optic fibre telephone lines – the shared resources that make the system work. The questions we want to address are: What does that infrastructure look like for organizational learning? What shared resources does the system need?

Before we propose a new infrastructure, we need to explain why the traditional infrastructure will not suffice. This traditional infrastructure is recognizable as the bureaucracy with its hierarchical levels, authority/compliance relationships, and specialized roles and tasks. Such an infrastructure is designed to move information, collected from lower levels, up through the hierarchical chain of command. It is, in effect, an infrastructure designed to facilitate the learning of those at the top. However, in moving information vertically rather than laterally, it works against the collective's ability to learn. While it may provide those at the top of the organization with the information necessary to make decisions, it does not take advantage of the sense-making capabilities that exist within the organization. Moreover, since the vertical flow of information makes those at the top the only ones with access to a composite picture of the whole system, it must be left to them to specify the actions of units throughout the organization and, likewise, to learn from the results of those actions. Thus all of the steps of the learning cycle are concentrated at the top. The traditional infrastructure simply does not have mechanisms in place to involve the collective, as a whole, in the learning cycle. As Chapters 4 and 5 illustrate, collective learning does not occur unless all members have full access to information, are able to view that information in terms of the context of the whole system, are able jointly to make sense of the information and choose actions based on that sense making, and then are able to observe the results of those actions so that they can improve.

We need a new kind of infrastructure to support organizational learning. To design such an infrastructure we return to the organizational learning cycle and ask ourselves what kind of infrastructure do we need to move us from each step to the next. The steps of the cycle become the poles that divide the cycle into four quadrants (see Figure 6.1).

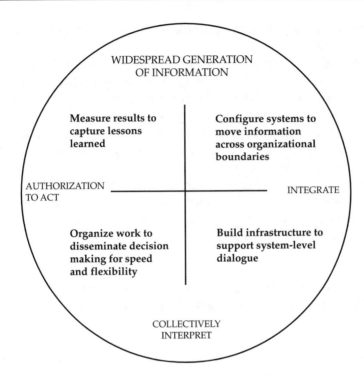

Figure 6.1   Infrastructure to support organizational learning

Starting at the top of the cycle, assuming 'widespread gener-ation of information' is occurring in an organization, what infrastructure is needed to allow that information to be inte-grated into the organizational context? The infrastructure in the first quadrant describes how to *configure systems to move information across organizational boundaries*.

For the second quadrant, assuming that organizational members are able to 'integrate their information into the organ-izational context', what infrastructure is needed to create an ongoing collective interpretation? The second quadrant describes an *infrastructure to support system-level dialogue*.

The third quadrant assumes that collective interpretation has been made and asks what infrastructure is needed to give organ-izational members 'authority to take action on the collective interpretation'? The third quadrant describes an infrastructure that *organizes work to disseminate decision making for speed and flexibility.*

Finally, the fourth quadrant assumes 'the local authority to take action' and asks what kind of infrastructure is necessary to allow local units to 'generate new information' from their actions, thus completing the cycle? The necessary infrastructure is a local process to *measure results to capture lessons learned.*

There is not 'one right way' to construct any one quadrant, rather there are many possible ways. In discussing each quadrant we will try first to describe it in general, secondly we will provide a number of examples from different organizations to illustrate the variety of ways it can be achieved and, finally, we will delineate its essential elements.

Quadrant 1 – Configure systems to move information across organizational boundaries

Quadrant 1 (see Figure 6.2) describes the infrastructure needed to move the information that was developed through the widespread generation of information, across organizational boundaries so that it can be accessed by others in the organization, and integrated into organizational members' understanding of their own work. The infrastructure might include multi-functional project teams, technology fairs, the co-location of project members, intranet inquiries, knowledge databases, joint meetings of departments, and network meetings, both electronic and face-to-face.

All of these facilitate members' ability to share knowledge that was learned locally across organizational boundaries. For some of these the sharing is a by-product of a more task-oriented goal, e.g. product development, while others are more deliberately aimed at sharing knowledge. The need for sharing knowledge is often explained as 'let's not reinvent the wheel' or the need to 'leverage our knowledge'. From a learning perspective, the knowledge that individuals (or teams) gain through their experience is a shared resource.

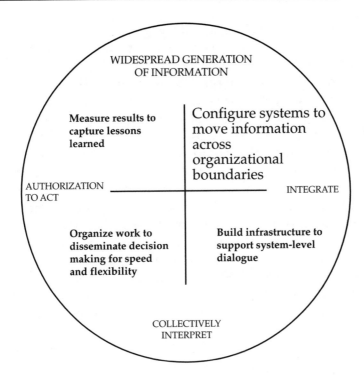

Figure 6.2   Quadrant 1 of the infrastructure

Our examples are drawn from a variety of organizations which have been intentional about creating infrastructure through which knowledge can be shared. Certainly new technology has been a great boon to this effort. Although not all of our examples rely on technology, we start with two examples that do.

The large consulting firms have been leaders in this effort, developing elaborate databases that contain information about consulting processes, clients, best practices, the expertise possessed by different consultants, and the current literature on specific topics. At Ernst & Young (E&Y), at the end of a consulting engagement, each team is required to submit its work products to a database. Senior consultants in each area or specialization have the responsibility of shifting through those submissions to cull out those that are exemplary. These become part of special electronic packages, 'Powerpacks', that other teams can use with clients. By making use of this shared knowledge, a consultant can reduce the time it takes to develop a customized proposal for a client from three weeks to three days, an enormous cost saving. The infrastructure that supports the consultants in the re-use of knowledge involves not only the databases but also knowledge stewards who sort and manage the submissions, the laptop computers which every consultant carries with him or her, the eight hundred telephone numbers which provide easy access to the databases from anywhere in the world, the frequent network meetings that bring together consultants who are doing similar work, the submission process which is designed to be quick and easy, and the commonality of software which means that learning one database gives easy access to all others. E&Y has developed an extensive infrastructure for learning with the ratio of knowledge worker to knowledge user of 1:100 and at a cost of 6 per cent of E&Y's sales dollar.

The learning infrastructure that Ford has developed is a 'push' rather than the 'pull' system of E&Y. Each of Ford's twenty-six Vehicle Operations plants automatically receives a small number of best practice items each week specifically targeted to Vehicle Operations. To qualify to be placed in the database, these best practices have already been implemented in sister plants and the dollar savings they achieved calculated. A designated production engineer in each plant is required to respond to each of the best practices that appear on the computer screen, indicating the disposition the plant has decided to make of that item, e.g. 'under investigation', 'adopted', 'not applicable'. The purpose of Ford's Best Practice Replication Process is to assist the plants to reach the 5 per cent productivity increase they are tasked with each year. The number of adoptions by each plant is tracked and displayed by the computer, as is the number of contributions of each plant to the database. Ford boasts $1.6 billion dollars in value added in a little over three years from the re-use of ideas developed in sister plants. The infrastructure that supports this effort comprises:

1   The database that distributes the best practices.
2   The designated production engineers in each plant who receive the items and in turn submit items.
3   Plant management meetings at which decisions are made about adoption.
4   The response and tracking system that produces and distributes reports of replication activity.
5   Frequent face-to-face meetings of production engineers from across Ford.
6   The plant productivity requirement which drives the continual search for new ideas to reduce cost.
7   A small central staff of half a dozen people who maintain the system and market it internally to other parts of Ford.

The two systems described above are designed to share explicit knowledge, that is, knowledge that can be written down and then retrieved for use by someone else. There is also a great need to share tacit knowledge, knowledge that is not easily codified or made explicit but that with an appropriate infrastructure can nevertheless be shared across organizational boundaries. British Petroleum (BP) has such a system in 'Peer Assist'.

'Peer Assist' allows a team that is working on a project to call upon another team, which has had experience in the same type of task (or a group of experienced individuals), to meet face-to-face for a period of one to three days to assist with an issue they are facing. For example, a team that is drilling in deep water off the coast of Norway can ask for an 'assist' from a team that has had experience in deep water drilling in the Gulf of Mexico. As the label implies, 'assists' are held between peers, not with supervisors or corporate 'helpers'. The idea of 'Peer Assists' was suggested by a corporate task force in late 1994 and BP wisely chose to offer it as a simple idea without specifying rules or lengthy 'how to' steps. It is left up to the team asking for the assist to identify who it wants, what it wants help on, and at what stage in the project it wants the help.

For BP the infrastructure has amounted to little more than the sanctioning of the idea by the corporate task force. In a highly decentralized organization, the 'Peer Assist' offers the team requesting the assistance a measure of assurance that they are not making an obvious or fatal mistake about what are often very costly actions they are undertaking. There is a built-in reward for those who do the 'assisting' as well, in that they have the opportunity to expand their own knowledge by addressing a familiar problem in a totally new context. The first few Peer Assists that were held received guidance from the initiating corporate task force, but teams quickly found the idea so useful that they began acting on their own initiative. Within three years after its inception almost a thousand BP teams called for a Peer Assist. The team sending assisters bears the cost of travel in order to simplify the paperwork, confident that others will reciprocate in due course. The infrastructure needed for this type of sharing is far simpler than the elaborate databases of Ford and E&Y, but it is nonetheless critical. The simple infrastructure in this BP example is a process with a recognizable name that labels it as sanctioned and that acknowledges the purpose it serves.

BP has a number of other methods of sharing knowledge, some of which are considerably more complex than Peer Assist. For example, a team, on-site at a rig, can hold an in-depth video conversation with peers on another continent to obtain immediate expert help on a specific problem that may have just occurred at the site. The infrastructure involved requires not only the equipment, but also enough face-to-face networking opportunities between engineers so that they know who to call for what problem. BP claims that video conferencing between sites has saved 30 million dollars through a reduction in person hours needed to solve problems, a decrease in helicopter trips to off-shore oil platforms, and a reduction in rework during construction projects.

Chevron spends over 5 billion dollars a year on capital projects. Because reducing cost in this area is critical, Chevron has established an infrastructure that connects managers on new projects to those who are facing similar issues on existing or past projects. At the start of a new project a project manager can make use of the services of an internal consultant from

Chevron's Project Resources Group, to help implement the best practice knowledge about capital project management from across Chevron. These internal consultants are human links that can connect project managers to capital projects within Chevron (at any time there may be over 200) from which they can learn. Although there are numerous databases available to these project managers, the real cost savings lies in having a human mind that fully comprehends the specifics of the context of a project, is equally aware of the specifics of other projects, *and* has the time and energy to make the connections. Sometimes all that is needed is a document that can be pulled up on the computer, other times the needed knowledge requires a site visit, a conference call, or a shared resource. The internal consultant works with a project manager off and on, over the life of a project, which might be up to two years, and is eventually able to use that project as a source of knowledge for newly developing projects. Chevron says that making these internal connections can save up to 20 per cent on the cost of a project. In the downstream operation, from 1992 to 1997 that amounted to 816 million dollars in savings, a testament to the ability of learning to impact the bottom line. Although the Project Resources Group was originally carried as overhead, it has evolved into a profit centre with some twenty consultants, each of whom specializes in a specific area of project management. This group supports a network of project managers, holds best practice seminars, manages the databases, and keeps up on the latest technology in the industry.

The US Army is another organization that has a number of tools to collect and move knowledge. One of the most innovative is the use of 'collectors'. Topics about which the Army needs new or additional knowledge are identified at a strategic level. A team of 'borrowed' experts within the identified topic areas are selected and trained as 'collectors'. Then when an operation occurs that has the potential for offering insight into the needed topic, the 'collectors' are sent, observing and collecting lessons on behalf of the Army as a whole. Events are observed as they occur and the descriptions are gathered in real time. The 'collectors' look for answers to recurring problems rather than those due to error or temporary anomalies. They collect multiple perspectives on each event and attempt to tease out tacit as well as explicit knowledge. However, the 'collectors' do more than gather information, they also act as information conduits – improving current operations on the ground by sharing solutions from memory, a kind of 'cross-talk'. The information they collect is sent to the Center for Army Lessons Learned (CALL) where it is examined by yet another group of experts and where it is translated into a variety of forms for re-use. The infrastructure for the Army is complex, involving the identification of targeted knowledge needs, the borrowing and training of collectors, an electronic network and digital photographic equipment that sends information back to CALL, a separate system of analysis with its personnel and distribution system, and the redistribution of knowledge through doctrine, training, and through the collectors themselves.

All of the examples cited so far are designed to share information horizontally. However, an infrastructure to share information vertically is also critical to this quadrant. Organizations have traditionally had fairly effective methods to send instructions and orders from senior management to those in lower ranks. The new infrastructure required in this quadrant is that which makes available to its members the key business indicators of the organization and then trains them on their importance and usefulness. Key business indicators are industry specific and the infrastructure for making them available is equally varied. Hewlett Packard puts its key business indicators in a database that is open and accessible to all organizational members on their desktop. This enables units to obtain the information they need, when they need it, whether from other units, senior management, or external sources. At Commercial Casework, a custom furniture builder, the key numbers (business indicators) are related to labour-hours, and they are posted on the lunchroom wall. At Sprint's Government Systems Division, a US telecommunication company, the key number is revenue per employee. At Manco, a consumer-products manufacturer, there are several key numbers including manufacturing direct support, dollars and percent of net sales. These numbers are displayed on running electric signs posted throughout the facility. For Pace Industries, a plant that makes die-cast metal parts, it is inventory accuracy and scrap reduction that is posted on the shopfloor. The infrastructure to accomplish this sharing of information is not complex, it is necessary, however, that it meet the qualities outlined in Chapter 5 of being accurate, timely and complete.

A second necessary part of the infrastructure is assisting organizational members to understand the information and to connect it to their own activities. This is particularly important when, as will be outlined in quadrant 3, organizational members have a financial stake in those numbers. In some companies 'business literacy' is taught to all organizational members so that they understand the way in which such things as inventory, inventory costs, purchasing variances, marketing expenses, etc. affect the bottom line. Some companies have accomplished this in creative ways, making games out of it or having learners create fictitious companies to learn from. When organizational members have a greater understanding of the numbers they are more likely to be able to assist in managing them, but also are more likely to question them. The second quadrant affords them that opportunity.

There are a number of essential elements of this first quadrant. The first is that the infrastructure provides multiple ways to share knowledge, not just relying on a single mechanism. For example, BP's knowledge-sharing infrastructure probably has fifteen different ways including, the databases, Peer Assist, and video conferencing from the rigs, discussed here. The second element is related to the first, the need for both face-to-face and technology-based processes. Those organizations that began their knowledge-sharing efforts with only technology have seen the need to add face-to-face components in order to make them function effectively. For example, Ford has a very sophisticated database, but it is the quarterly meetings of production engineers that builds the necessary trust so that the database is used. A third essential element is that these processes are tied to specific business goals. For example, Chevron's Project Management Resources is intended to reduce capital costs. Such processes are not designed to share knowledge in the abstract, but rather toward a designated and valued end. And finally, these processes are designed by the users. At Ford, the initial system was a paper product that production engineers traded among themselves. When it was placed on a computer database, the production engineers identified what information they needed from each other, how it should be displayed, and what the criteria should be for submission.

Quadrant 2 – Build infrastructure to support system-level dialogue

Quadrant 2 (see Figure 6.3) describes the kind of infrastructure needed to bring the knowledge embedded within the parts of the system together so that collective sense can be made of what is known.

As with the examples described for the first quadrant, there are a variety of ways to construct such an infrastructure. Some of these are 'whole system in the room' processes such as WorkOut (GE), Strategic Search Conferences (Weisbord, 1992), Real Time Strategic Change (Jacobs, 1994), Open Space Technology (Owen, 1991), the Conference Model (Emery, 1993), and Team Syntegrity (Beer, 1994).

'Whole system in the room' processes bring from 80–300 organizational members together with representatives from suppliers and customers for a three- to five-day meeting. Much of the work is done in small groups alternating between functional and mixed groups. The meetings are facilitated by outside professionals and follow developed processes to systematically generate and test ideas. As an example, in 1993, Whole Foods, a natural food grocery chain, used Weisbord's process of a Strategic Search Conference in a three-day event that brought together over seventy people representing store managers, employees, customers and suppliers. One of the issues Whole Foods had been struggling with was whether to continue its

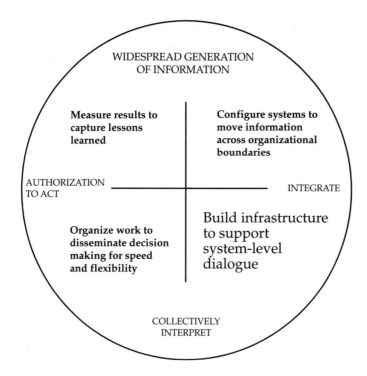

Figure 6.3   Quadrant 2 of the infrastructure

rapid expansion. Many of the current store managers were opposed to continued expansion, valuing the benefits of a relatively small-sized organization. However, from the discussions during the three days it became clear to the store managers that continued growth was essential to the long-term viability of the chain. The store managers' change in perspective came as a result of the reasoning they themselves worked through in discussion with other voices in the conference. It was reflected in the target the Conference set, 100 stores and 1 billion dollars in sales by 1998. Another learning that grew out of the Conference came from hearing the vendors speak about how difficult the chain was to deal with because there was no common voice. Neither corporate nor store managers had been aware of this vendor concern before the Conference. As a result of this new knowledge the chain established a national purchasing director.

Many of the outcomes of the conference were direct, such as the change in store manager perspective and centralized buying, but an equal number were like seeds that were planted by what was learned in the conference and would grow into action plans later on, often at the local level.

Team Syntegrity, originated by Stafford Beer (1994), is based on the polyhedral geometry of Buckminster Fuller. The process brings together thirty participants from different parts of the organization around a topic that requires breakthrough thinking. The thirty identify twelve themes important to the topic. The group holds a sequence of meetings based on the 'nodes' of the polyhedron, so that by the end of the three- to five-day period thirty-six meetings (the 36 sides of the polyhedron) have been held to explore the twelve topics. The quintessential feature is that eleven of the twelve themes are represented in every meeting, so that not only are diverse per- spectives brought to bear on the topics, but the relationship of the topics to each other is thoroughly examined. The configur- ation of the repeated discussions creates a synergy around key ideas and work to prevent the ideas of high status persons from dominating. The result is innovative ideas that grow out of the collective interpretation as well as a commitment to move forward in the directions the group has developed. Follow-up meetings in the work site again make use of the polyhedral configuration to maintain the momentum and alignment of the initial meeting.

An example of the use of Team Syntegrity is a small employee-owned (200 owners) building materials company on the US Eastern seaboard. The company was facing a series of challenges that were perceived as 'life and death' issues – although senior management was having trouble getting action to happen on several that had been identified for a couple of years. Competition and technology had changed the nature of the marketplace and the size of the competition. The com- pany's values and spirit of shared ownership were becoming clouded by the pressure of business and the bad habits that develop when there are too many crises and not enough players. The topic of the three-and-a-half day Syntegration was how to build on the company's unique culture to make it a leader in the building materials industry. The thirty participants who met off site were a cross-section of the company, ranging from the president to a truck driver. Some of the important ideas and action steps that resulted from the meeting were:

- change the structure of Board of Directors to protect against share sell-outs
- create an Employee Council with the mandate to gather information and advise the board on any issue employee/owners felt necessary
- a Profit Leak Detection and Correction system
- buy-in by chief financial officer and managers to Open Book management
- a Customer Service Improvement process.

As is often the case, none of these directions was foreseen or advocated by the Syntegration facilitators (Beatty, 1998). Following the initial Syntegration, participants held meetings in every location the first week back and the nomination process for Employee Council began. Plans were put in place to hire an expert resource to support the forward movement of the culture on several fronts. Training programmes to acquaint newcomers (and old timers) with the value-based management system were designed. Syntegration has been used with corporations as well as non-governmental agencies working on environmental and peace issues.

The idea of bringing large groups of people together for several days may seem incongruous at a time when organizational members are increasingly dispersed, with teams often being only virtual and increasing numbers of employees who are telecommuting or 'hoteling'. But we believe that in a time when work is virtual and members are geographically dispersed, there is a heightened need for periodic times of 'high-touch', for collective interpretation. Rather than the co-location of the past, the new infrastructure may require organizational members to oscillate between geographic dispersion and periodic large group meetings or coordinated organization-wide dialogues.

A different type of infrastructure to support system-level dialogue makes use of the team as the unit of learning. Learning Maps such as those designed by Root Learning are graphic illustrations of an issue with which an organization is dealing. The graphic illustrations are printed as wall-size maps. Across the organization, teams (either intact or cross-functional) meet around the graphic for two- to four-hour discussions of the issues illustrated. Graphic illustrations, being more ambiguous than words, provide a focus for a very rich discussion, and yet allow for a wide-range of ideas to emerge. A trucking company of some 6000 people at 90 remote sites, used learning maps to help them change their strategy from a long-haul carrier to two short-haul carriers. Over a period of less than a month, the whole organization focused on this critical issue and the implications it had for each part. Through the group discussions organizational members came to their own conclusions which they then took responsibility to act upon.

As with the examples described in quadrant 1, to be effective these processes have to be recognizable by name and identified as ways to have system-wide dialogue. They have to become part of the culture of the organization. That means they cannot be one-off events, used once to remedy a specific problem. When General Electric (GE) began to use WorkOut (Welch, 1992) in the early 1990s it was an 'event' that required someone like a trained facilitator that knew how to do it. After some ten years of use, it is a way work gets done at GE. When a problem arises that cuts across functions, organizational members are likely to say, 'We'd better call a WorkOut on this'. They know how to do WorkOut, when it is needed and what kind of results they can expect from it. This sort of shaping of the culture does not happen overnight, but when these kinds of processes are introduced over time they begin to shape the culture, which in turn changes the way organizational members think about how they work.

As can be seen from the examples, there are many types of infrastructure that can be used to support system-level dialogue. In Chapter 3 the characteristics of Hallways were discussed at some length. Since what we have been describing as the infrastructure to support system-level dialogue could just as easily be called 'Hallways' those same characteristics are applicable to this quadrant. To review them briefly, they are: dialogue-based meetings rather than those where presentations are made, designed to give equal weight to all voices, and for this reason are non-management facilitated, involve multiple perspectives, and are unpredictable as to outcome.

Quadrant 3 – Organize work to disseminate decision making for speed and flexibility

Quadrant 3 (see Figure 6.4) deals with the need to translate collective interpretation into local action. As with the other

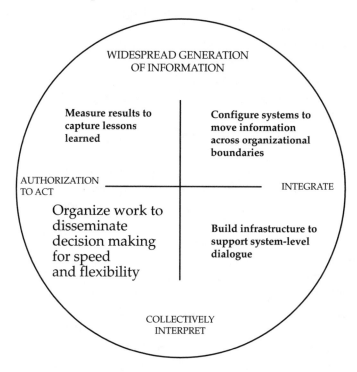

Figure 6.4 Quadrant 3 of the infrastructure

quadrants there are many types of infrastructure that can accomplish this translation.

Regardless of the type, three critical elements seem to be necessary:

1   Some level of local autonomy.
2   Local units having a financial stake in the organization's success.
3   Keeping the size of the local unit small.

Organizations have been talking about local autonomy for a number of years. The rise of self-managed or self-directed work teams are testament to the interest in local autonomy. The infrastructure for quadrant 3 needs to provide enough autonomy that teams or small business units can act on what they observe and learn, with enough coordination that their local actions work together toward the collective goal rather than producing organizational chaos. This autonomy can best be achieved through a decentralized structure that makes teams or small business units self-managing. The coordination is achieved through the 'integration of information' and the 'collective interpretation'. The local action that units take is, in a very real way, authorized by the collective understanding that has been achieved.

There are many examples from across the globe. The Baltimore plant of Chesapeake Packaging Company makes corrugated boxes. It is made up of eight internal companies: Quality Trucking which handles shipping, Chesapeake Maintenance Services maintains the machinery, Corrugator Specialties Unlimited is responsible for the corrugating process, and so on. Each 'company' has an elected president that rotates from within the company every six months. These internal companies compile their own operating information and are responsible for managing their own affairs. Once a month everyone in the plant meets to review the numbers and build an income statement (collective interpretation). If the plant hits a certain target level of earnings, profit-sharing kicks in and employees receive a bonus of at least 5 per cent of their gross monthly income, with the percentages rising as the profits rise.

Published Image Inc. produces newsletters for financial-service companies. It is made up of many self-organizing work teams, each with its own editor, art director, salesperson and staffers, and they function like self-contained businesses. Each collects its own receivables and keeps its own books. The company-wide compensation system provides rewards commensurate with team-level business success.

Increasingly we are seeing large organizations create infrastructure based on the concepts of federalism. British Petroleum, for example, restructured to this form in 1990. Royal Dutch Shell and Unilever did so decades ago. Federal models provide a way to take advantage of the large size that is essential for a global presence, while also gaining the innovation, flexibility and sense of community that are the benefits of being small. Federalism differs markedly from decentralization. With decentralization the centre or corporate headquarters delegates certain tasks or duties to units, while remaining in overall control. By contrast, with federalism, the centre's power is given to it by the outlying groups in a sort of reverse delegation – the centre doesn't control – but coordinates and it does so only with the consent of the units. The difference is more than semantics, it is the difference in where power is located (Handy, 1995).

Subsidiarity is the most important of federalism's principles. It asserts that power rightfully belongs to the lowest possible point in the organization where it can be carried out. In the United States power resides in the States, but likewise, the State should not attempt to do what the family can do better. When BP became a federation, corporate devolved authority and responsibility to its separate businesses retaining for itself a list of twenty-two 'reserve powers'. However, after discussions with the now separate businesses, these were reduced to ten. The business units 'consented' to a much smaller number of 'reserve powers' than corporate had at first thought necessary to retain.

One of the ways interdependence is achieved between the separate business units in many federalist companies is to locate services or facilities needed by all in the territory of one or two. Bechtel is a multi-billion dollar international engineering corporation, with 18 000 employees worldwide. All Power Generation projects (fossil, nuclear, renewable) are started in the Power Center of Excellence in Gaithersburg, Maryland, no matter where in the world the plant will be constructed. It is here that Bechtel's knowledge and expertise about power generation is held and grown. Houston and London are the Centers of Excellence for Petrochemical projects and San Francisco is the Center of Excellence for Government business. Having many centres of expertise, rather than one central source, creates a distribution of power and makes interdependence a reality.

The second element of this infrastructure, making certain that local units have a stake in the organization's success, can be accomplished by a variety of group incentives such as bonus plans, profit sharing and stock distribution. For any of these to function effectively:

1   The members of the unit must have a clear understanding of how their actions relate to the payout.
2   They must be able to affect the outcome by their own efforts.
3   The numbers on which the payout is based must be available to the organizational members.

Having a stake in the organization's success is unquestionably an incentive issue, but it is just as importantly an equity issue. When organizational members share their ideas with others in the organization, struggle with others to make collective meaning, and actively seek out new ideas from external sources, they no longer see themselves as just hired hands. They begin to view themselves as partners in the enterprise, and as partners they expect to be compensated when their efforts (behaviour or knowledge, actions or ideas) bring about exceptional results. Compensation tied directly to the accomplishments of the local units is a recognition of the investment they have made of their own ingenuity and knowledge. In many of these organizations members receive a base pay that is considerably lower than industry standards. They also receive pay based on how well their local unit functioned (sometimes as much as 20 per cent of their total compensation) and they receive additional pay based on the total corporation's surplus, again sometimes as much as 20 per cent. In good years the total take home pay of these organization members far exceeds industry standards, and in poor years no one is laid off to reduce costs, because the costs are reduced automatically.

The third element that makes this infrastructure work is keeping the size small. The number of people any organizational member can feel connected and responsible to is limited. Chaparral Steel thinks 1000 is the upper limit. Other organizations deliberately keep their number closer to 500, believing that when the community is much larger individuals lose their sense of connection to each other and to the whole. W. L. Gore limits plants to 150 people. Perhaps most critically when organizations are large their members are apt to lose the sense that what they do matters. It is hard to establish a productive working relationship to faceless or numerous others, people that are never seen and only known as 'them'. Willingness to ask others for help or to care enough about others to offer help requires a sense of connection with those others – a relationship. Organizational learning is dependent on being able to gain a sense of the whole.

To reiterate, the three essential elements of this infrastructure are:

1 Some level of local autonomy that is grounded in collective interpretation.
2 Local units having a financial stake in the organization's success.
3 Keeping the size of the local unit small enough that organizational members can be in a relationship to each other.

Of the four quadrants the infrastructure suggested for this one would appear to have the most consequential political impact. In fact, some might question why the size, structure and reward systems of the organization are considerations for organizational learning. It is possible that they do bear little relationship to *individual* learning, but they are clearly at the very heart of collective learning. Organizations such as Chaparral Steel, Johnsonville Foods, Harley Davidson, Shell Oil, British Petroleum, that are actively and successfully moving in the direction of collective learning, find themselves also moving toward greater local autonomy, changes in the reward system and finding ways to reduce the effects of size.

Quadrant 4 – Measure results to capture lessons learned

When local units are given the autonomy to act on the collective interpretation there must also be an infrastructure in place that provides a way for the members of those units to be accountable for both their processes and their outcomes (see Figure 6.5).

Unit members themselves need to design measures that are specific to their own processes. Meyer (1994) has described one such methodology as 'dashboards' and says, 'trying to run a team without a good, simple guidance system is like trying to drive a car without a dashboard' (p.96). He points out that it is critical that such measures are 'owned' by the unit rather than by higher management.

Being 'owned' means the measures are designed, collected and used by the unit to make decisions about what actions to take and how to correct their course; being 'owned' by the unit also means that the dashboard measures are not used primarily as a reporting tool to higher management. Clearly each unit must have some outcome measures which do serve a reporting function. But it is difficult for the same set of numbers to usefully serve both improvement and reporting functions; difficult because the more useful dashboard measures are designed to identify errors and problems in the unit's processes and if unit members knew those numbers were to be reported upward they would be more likely to design measures that gave a favourable impression rather than a useful assessment. Organizational learning requires that local units make mistakes together and

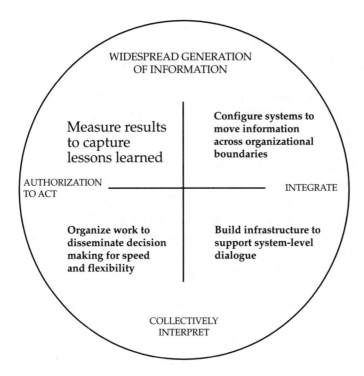

Figure 6.5 Quadrant 4 of the infrastructure

clean up the mess together without recriminations from above. The numbers help units identify those mistakes.

Meyer tells the story of a team in a Europe-based car company that was charged with improving the total service process from product breakdown through repair. The team reviewed the existing measure – how often parts ordered by dealers could be filled from the warehouse shelf – but saw it as providing little data with which to improve the processes. Because the new team was responsible for the entire process, it mapped all the steps in the service cycle from the moment the warehouse received a dealer's order to the moment the dealer received the part, and the time each step took. The team then identified its critical tasks and capabilities, which included the order-entry operation, the management-information system for tracking orders and inventories, warehouse operations, and shipping.

The team created cycle-time measures for six to eight sub-processes, which helped it see how much time was being spent on each step of the process relative to the value of that process. With this information, the team could begin figuring out how to reduce cycle time without sacrificing quality. Within six months, the team was able to reduce the service cycle considerably.

To develop the measures that will inform their actions, teams may need the help of measurement experts or basic training in how to construct useful measurement systems. As described in Chapter 4, at Johnsonville Foods, Management Information Systems was renamed 'Member Information Systems', to reflect the change in the function's customer base – from top management to local units. Local units are able to call on this function to help them design the measures that are specific to their own needs.

The dashboard measures described above are critical information, but there is also the need to 'make sense' of the numbers by unit members reflecting together about the relationship between their actions and the measurements. Numbers without interpretation and reflection do not improve action.

One of the organizations that has led the way in this area has been the US Army. 'After Action Reviews' (AARs) occur routinely at the end of any team or unit action. AARs enable the unit to learn from what has happened (good or bad) and to re-use those lessons immediately in the next battle or project. AARs are attended by all of the individuals, regardless of rank, who were engaged in the effort. The simple guidelines for holding AARs are:

1   No sugar coating.
2   Discover ground truth.
3   No thin skins.
4   Take notes.
5   Call it like you see it.

The learning from these meetings is captured on three levels:

1 Individuals write and keep their own personal notes about what each needs to do differently.

2 They discuss how the unit, as a whole, functioned and what it needed to do differently in the next engagement, which is then recorded.

3 For certain engagements that have been identified as strategic, lessons learnt are sent to the Center for Army Lessons Learned (CALL) to be made available system-wide.

'After Action Reviews' typically focus on three key questions: What happened in the engagement? What was supposed to happen? and What accounts for the difference?

British Petroleum has yet another example of an infrastructure that facilitates a team or unit in examining its processes. At BP 'completion meetings' are a part of any project management process so the project is not done until one has been held. Output from completion meetings includes lessons learnt, action points (with an assigned owner) and quantification (internal measures such as completion time, under budget, time for critical path items and satisfaction ratings). A critical part of the completion meetings is a 'lessons learnt' discussion. These discussions include all team members, the project leader, and the customer, who is often from the next highest level of the organization. 'Lessons learnt' meetings last from half an hour to half a day, depending upon the number of people and scope. Unlike the US Army's AARs, an external facilitator is key for the BP meetings. Using his/her questioning skills the facilitator helps the group move beyond symptoms to cause. When projects are lengthy or are umbrella projects, BP holds six-monthly 'lessons learnt' meetings as well as the completion meeting.

Meetings such as the US Army's AARs and BP's 'lessons learnt' meetings are a local level version of the collective interpretation, thus the same characteristics apply; a time of reflection and dialogue, not speeches, egalitarian participation not polite response to authority, and the encouragement of multiple perspectives rather than like minds.

The infrastructure for this quadrant consists of measurement tools designed by the local unit, the availability of assistance in constructing such tools, and a process for unit reflection (again named and recognizable) that facilitates the unit learning from mistakes as well as successes. This infrastructure is necessary at several levels of the organization. The examples mentioned have been at the team or project level, although it is as critical at the department, or small business unit level. At any level where organizational members work together collaboratively to accomplish a goal, there is need for measures and processes for collectively reflecting on those measures.

The critical elements of quadrant 4 are, first, the local design of measures that allow the unit to track and improve its own performance and, when needed, design assistance. Secondly, that the measures the local unit constructs are related to the overall measures and goals of the organization. Thirdly, that the members of the local unit come together to make sense of the numbers and to determine what they need to do to improve those numbers. Finally, that what is learned or gained from those meetings is made available to others across the organization, which is, of course, a part of the first quadrant.

Getting started

Many organizations already have put one or two parts of this infrastructure in place and by doing so have gained considerable learning and improved productivity. They may, for example, have a knowledge database for sharing lessons learned (quadrant 1) or they may hold frequent 'all hands' meetings to help integrate what is going on in the separate parts of the organization (quadrant 2). But without all four parts of the infrastructure they do not maximize collective learning. Having one part of the infrastructure in place is like building a magnificent sports facility without building the roads that will carry the traffic to and from it. To bring the analogy back to organizations, if local units are functioning autonomously in order to get the flexibility and speed that the organization needs (quadrant 3), but those local units have no sense of how they are integrated with other units (quadrant 2), they are likely to sub-optimize decisions; if departments are sharing knowledge learned from their experiences (quadrant 1) but that knowledge is not backed up by numbers and proven results (quadrant 4), organizational members are likely to devalue the knowledge and the system that supports it. Each of these four quadrants represents an essential part of the infrastructure that makes the cycle work – that makes organizational learning happen.

That said, there is still the question of where to start. There are, as usual, two starting points, local units or a centralized group. When the interest is within local units the best place to begin is with the first or fourth quadrants. The first quadrant, 'configure systems to move information across organizational boundaries', most often targets people involved in a specific type of work who need to share knowledge with each other, e.g. production engineers at Ford. Although the knowledge users may be geographically dispersed, they usually already have some minimal communication network set up that can form the basis for lateral cooperation to achieve a more delib-erate knowledge-sharing infrastructure. Recently, for example, the HR community at Lockheed Martin took the initiative to build an infrastructure to share HR best practices across its 200 plus companies. Other local units have reconfigured their physical space to make sharing knowledge more likely. In other organizations teams have met with their supplier or customer teams to see what useful knowledge they can get and give.

The fourth quadrant, 'measure results to capture lessons learned', is also a place to initiate action on a local or regional level. BP's Project Management Lessons Learnt programme is a case in point. The programme was started by one of the subsidi-aries, Norway Emerging Areas (NEA), because that group saw it as a way to reduce workload by learning from each other. It has since spread to other parts of BP, but its beginning was among sixty project managers who met together to agree upon a process they believed would benefit them all. Likewise, the development of local measures, or a 'dashboard' that can provide information from which a group can learn can be done at a local plant level, team level or project group level. It takes that group meeting together to devise useful measures, collecting the data on a regular basis and holding morning meetings or weekly meetings to make sense of the numbers.

Quadrants 2 and 3 require the most coordination – 'build infrastructure to support system-level dialogue' and 'organize work to disseminate decision making for speed and flexibility' – because of their implications for realignment of power and, for 3, the realignment of rewards as well. Since, in most organizations, corporate holds the power, their involvement and consent is required to share that power.

When the organizational learning initiative is begun at a corporate or central level then quadrant 2 is a good place to start. An organization might begin with the 'whole system in the room' for a strategic planning effort. The Bank of Montreal, for example, began experimenting with Open Space meetings and now holds Open Space three or four times a year in various forms and configurations. 'Whole system in the room' meetings are, of course, only a beginning, but in many organizations such meetings have sown the necessary seeds for organizational learning to begin to grow.

References

Beatty, D. J. F. (1998) *Personal correspondence*. Toronto, Canada.

Beer, S. (1994). *Beyond Dispute: The Invention of Team Syntegrity*. New York: Wiley.

Emery, M. (ed.) (1993). *Participative Design for Participative Democracy*. Centre for Continuing Education, Australian National University.

Handy, C. (1995). *Beyond Certainty: The Changing Worlds of Organisations*. Random House (UK) Limited.

Jacobs, R. (1994). *Real Time Strategic Change*. San Francisco: Berrett-Koehler.

Meyer, C. (1994). 'How the right measures help teams excel'. *Harvard Business Review*, **72** (3), 95–101.

Owen, H. (1991). *Riding the Tiger: Doing Business in a Transforming World*. Potomac, MD, Abbott Publishing.

Weisbord, M. (1992). *Discovering Common Ground*. San Francisco: Berrett-Koehler.

Welch, J. F. (1992). 'Working out of a tough year'. *Executive Excellence*, **9** (4), 14–16.

7 Measuring organizational learning

I feel a bit embarrassed to be writing this chapter because I am *not* writing about 'how to do it', but rather why it is not feasible to determine whether organizational learning makes a difference to the bottom line. Certainly a less popular subject! There is no doubt that as organizational learning gains credence with organizations there is a great demand to prove that it results in improved organizational performance. But we fool ourselves and others when we make that kind of claim. We can certainly measure a great many things about organizational learning, including whether processes are in place that facilitate learning, whether individuals in the organization are learning, the extent to which knowledge is being shared, the gains in saving made from that sharing, and whether units are acting in new or different ways. With good measurement techniques we can obtain valid data on such elements.

However, to make the claim that those elements result in improved organizational performance would require taking into account several layers of causal relationships. And with so many layers it would be unlikely we could 'prove' the outcome even in the most carefully constructed experimental setting – and certainly unlikely in the real world setting of organizations.

To explain the difficulties in measuring outcomes based on causal relationships, the assumed relationship between the most common elements of organizational learning is shown in Figure 7.1. The four boxes each represent an element of organizational learning. The arrows between the boxes indicate causation.

First, I will provide a brief overview of the chain of logic and then discuss both the logic and the elements in greater depth. I will start with the second box, which indicates that a needed outcome is that organizational members, both individually and collectively, will have gained 'knowledge'. For that to happen the organization needs to have in place factors which facilitate learning, e.g. open communication, participative decision making. These 'factors' are represented in the first box. The first causal relationship in the figure is that the facilitating factors will result in organizational members obtaining new knowledge. The third box shows that new or revised organizational 'action' is taken, with the causal relationship being that it was the knowledge that resulted in the organizational action. The fourth box indicates that improved organizational 'outcomes' have been achieved, and that this was caused by the new or revised action. To clarify the measurement issues it is necessary to consider *both* a measure of the outcomes (represented in each box) and to assure ourselves of the validity of the causal relationships between the boxes, because it is this chain of logic that is the basis for any attempt at proof of organizational learning.

Facilitating factors

In order for organizational members to learn, both individually and collectively, the organization has to put into place factors that facilitate learning. Few would argue that some organizational conditions promote increased learning (e.g. the availability of information, participative decision making) and

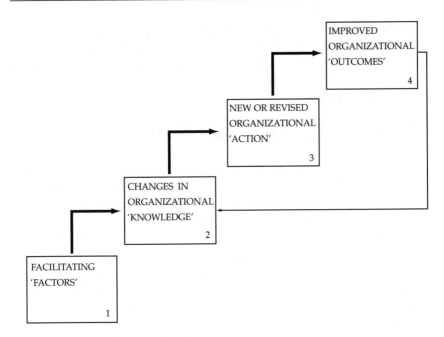

Figure 7.1 Causal relationships assumed in measuring organizational learning

that likewise some conditions prevent or limit learning, (e.g. organizational stovepipes, teams being too busy to draw out the lessons learned from a recent experience). Organizations which aspire to increase learning endeavour to put into practice those factors that facilitate learning, while eliminating those that lessen learning.

Measurement issues

Most of the surveys on the market today that purport to measure organizational learning, measure items in the factors box. The specific items and topics that are included in a survey depend on the theoretical framework of the survey designers, for example, some might lean more heavily toward communication issues while others might focus on business processes. Regardless of the specific items, these surveys measure process rather than outcome, in that they do not measure learning itself, either at the individual or organizational level; rather they measure organizational members' perception of the extent to which the factors that facilitate learning are in place. This is a useful measure, as long as it is not confused with measuring the extent to which an organization is learning.

Causal relationships between factors and knowledge

The first causal relationship in the diagram implies that if such facilitating factors are in place, organizational members, individually and in groups, will gain new knowledge. And it is generally held that the more of these facilitating factors an organization employs, the more extensive the learning that would occur. There is, however, a caution that needs to be raised about the validity of this causal relationship. There are a number of ways organizational members and groups might gain new knowledge that are unrelated to the facilitating factors that the organization might put into place, e.g. a particularly impactful new book on the market, a newly formed professional group, new employees bringing in new knowledge. Except in the most controlled conditions it would be difficult to attribute new knowledge exclusively to the facilitating factors. Thus, we could not say with any assurance that if increased knowledge occurred, it necessarily resulted from certain factors being in place. Likewise, if little or no increase in knowledge occurred, could we not say with assurance that the organization did not have facilitating factors in place.

Changes in organizational knowledge

The second box references changes in the knowledge of organizational members and groups as a result of the organization employing the facilitating factors. Three types of changes in knowledge might be expected to result:

1   Changes in the knowledge of organizational members, e.g.
    * more knowledge about the other parts of the organization

with which a unit is interdependent making it possible to take that interdependence into account in actions and decisions

- increased knowledge about how to improve a team's or individual's task
- increased understanding of how a task relates to the overall organizational goal
- greater knowledge of best practices in other areas that might be applicable to one's own area
- reframed understanding of specific problems (perspective that alters how a problem is viewed).

2 Changes in the degree to which knowledge is collective, e.g.

- greater concurrence about appropriate ends and means (shared meaning)
- reduction in the equivocality of issues (more agreement as to what actions and their results mean)
- fewer topics that are undiscussable within the organizational context.

3 The validity of that knowledge, e.g.

- the degree to which conclusions (inferences) are publicly tested
- the degree to which conclusions (inferences) are supported by data.

Measurement issues

These three issues are critical types of knowledge that organizations strive for. This section will address how it is possible to determine whether such knowledge has been gained. First, it would be necessary to show that the knowledge that organizational members formulate about relevant organizational issues and tasks has changed from time 'A' to time 'B'. This time dimension is a crucial element of learning; something has been learned only when it was not known at time 'A' and is known at time 'B'. It is the difference between 'A' and 'B' that we call learning or changes in knowledge as it is referenced in box 2.

The accepted ways to measure knowledge are either through tests, such as in a classroom, or interviews with learners to determine what they have learned. It is also possible to look at the behaviour of the learners, but that places the measurement in box 3, action. Behaviour is assumed to be the result of the knowledge rather than the knowledge itself.

For organizational learning, the use of tests is not feasible because most of the learning is from experience and it is not possible to know ahead of time what the experience will teach the learners, making a comparison of time 'A' and time 'B' not possible. Moreover, what is learned from an experience differs from individual to individual and group to group. Both attributes of learning from experience make tests a poor measure of learning that has resulted from work experience.

The most viable measurement process is some form of interview or group discussion about what was learned. Through After Action Reviews (AARs), such as the US Army employs, or Lessons Learnt meetings used by British Petroleum (see Chapter 6), it is possible to identify what knowledge a group has gained from a work experience. However, an interesting side effect is that the group reflection itself is likely to increase or alter the knowledge that has been learned! Such an outcome would presumably be viewed as an asset rather than a detriment, although it nevertheless invalidates the results in strict measurement terms.

The same issue is present when interviewing individuals about what they have learned. One such attempt on my part (Dixon, 1997) was to conduct interviews with task force members following a six-week effort to examine the product development cycle of a large computer company. The interviewer (in this case, paired task force members) asked questions about what the interviewees had learned in four categories: the product development process in the company; the organization itself; teamwork; and the interviewees themselves. During the interviews organizational members often began their response to a category by saying, 'Well, I'm not sure I learned very much about . . .' But as the interview proceeded they began to uncover the learning they had made – they were, in effect, learning in the process of reflecting on what they had done. They were putting together ideas and connections during the interview!

In addition to simple interviews there are more controlled

processes that can be employed; processes in which accuracy is given primacy. The Self-Q interview (Bougon, 1983) is one such technique. It maps cause and effect relationships of a respondent related to a specific issue. It displays a person's ends, means, conflicts, and contexts for sensemaking. Because of the concern that researcher bias may influence the process of uncovering the maps, Bougon has invented a non-directive interview process that involves four successive interviews (Lee, Courtney and O'Keefe, 1992; Bougon, 1983; Weick and Bougon, 1986).

Though often time consuming and somewhat invasive, it is nevertheless possible to measure the knowledge box. Although it might not be advisable to do so across the whole of an organization, it would be very useful to make such measurements in selected situations, the findings of which might be extrapolated to the larger organization. In fact, such measurements could provide important data for understanding what knowledge is, and is not, being gained and where new emphasis and resources need to be placed.

Causal relationships between knowledge and action

The causal relationship between knowledge and action implies that new knowledge of individuals and groups leads to new organizational action – that, in effect, organizational members act on what they have learned. There are two cautions about this causal relationship. First, it is possible for organizational members to learn things which they cannot figure out how to put to use in the organization or which they may not have the time or energy to put to use. So knowledge may have been gained but no new action result. Secondly, organizational members may take new organizational action for reasons other than having acquired new knowledge, e.g. former actions may no longer be possible; new regulations may require new action; political considerations may alter actions.

Thus we could have valid data showing that knowledge has been gained and valid data showing that new actions have been taken, without being able to prove that the one led to the other.

New or altered organizational action

The action box represents action taken on the basis of new knowledge that has been gained. Such new actions might include:

- strategy change
- process changes
- new products
- change in the organization's policy on the environment.

These are changes that are observable – we are able to observe a group or individual acting in new ways.

Measurement issues

Again time serves as a criteria, in that the action at time 'B' must be different from that which was taken at time 'A'. The measurement (or observation) of new action is less problematical than the attempt to measure gains in knowledge. As an example of measuring action, it is possible to observe that a unit has implemented flex time; that the company has changed its strategy to focus on business solutions rather than selling equipment; or that a new product was introduced. The difficulties come in 'when' and 'how much'. For example, if the knowledge gained (knowledge box) is that 'customers are better served by multi-disciplinary teams rather than by individual sales representatives', and subsequent action is taken to create such teams, the question arises 'At what point in the change-over process is the new action counted or measured?' At the decision point? After teams have formed? After teams have learned how to work well together? The 'how much' relates to what percentage of the representatives have to be formed into teams to say that the strategy has been implemented. When all individual representatives are members of teams? When teams are in key accounts? Again, these issues are only pertinent if *proof* of organizational learning is required. If the criteria is less than 'proof' then these differentiations are less critical.

Having identified the difficulties of measurement, I again want to advocate that, in spite of the difficulties, measures of the action box are critical to improving practice. In Chapter 6 one of the quadrants is 'Measure results to capture lessons learned'. There we advocate that local units need to develop measures to determine if their actions are achieving the outcomes for which they are designed. In that chapter there are several useful examples of measuring action – certainly, the Best Practice Replication Process at Ford is an exemplary model, although in a fairly specialized setting.

Causal relationships between action and outcome
The causal relationship between the boxes for action and outcome implies that the action that groups or individuals take is responsible for changes in organizational performance. Even more cautions need to be raised for this relationship. Perhaps the most obvious is that system theory has made it apparent that many factors affect organizational outcomes – the reality of multiple causation. Concomitant changes such as new competitors, market changes, and increased or reduced materials cost make it difficult to assign causation to one factor.

In addition, March and Olsen (1976) warn that organizations are subject to 'superstitious learning'. This occurs when, because of propinquity, the assumption is made that a certain action produced a result when, in fact, the result was unrelated to the action. The apocryphal story of the athlete who insists on wearing a favoured pair of socks to every race, because they were worn when he or she won the gold medal, illustrates 'superstitious learning'.

A still further caution from Senge (1990) is that organizational outcomes are often both time and space delayed. For example, it may take some outcomes a year or more to manifest themselves; and outcomes may occur in parts of the system that are quite distant from the action and therefore may be difficult to detect.

Organizational outcomes

The outcomes box represents changes in organizational performance. This box is perhaps the easiest to measure, particularly in regard to financial measures, but increasingly also in regard to a more balanced scorecard (Kaplan and Norton, 1996). The difficulties then, are not in the measurement of the box, but in the causal relationship between the action box and the outcome box that has just been discussed.

Causal relationships between outcomes and knowledge
There is a final feedback loop in Figure 7.1 from the outcomes box back to the knowledge box. The assumption is that by tracking the improved (or decreased) organizational performance, knowledge is gained about what organizational action 'worked' and what new action to take. All of the cautions that applied to the causal relationship between the action box and the outcomes box are also of concern here. To say the least, this is a difficult relationship to prove.

Using measurement for learning

I conclude through this lengthy explanation, that although it is possible and useful to make a fairly rigorous measurement of any one of the four boxes, the causal relationships between the boxes are too tenuous to have confidence in them as *proof* of organizational learning. I do not want to imply that we should conclude that organizations are not learning or that the efforts to improve learning in organizations are not productive. Rather, the fault lies with the complexities within which organizations are embedded (multiple causation, outcomes that are time and space delayed, many different programmes and processes initiated within the same time frame); paradoxically, if this complexity did not exist, organizations would not be in such great need of organizational learning.

Using measurement for learning

Measurement has a critical role to play in organizational learning, although it is not the role of proof. We need to think of measurement in a different way, more akin to the way the quality movement has used measurement – to increase our understanding of how our processes are working and, on the basis of valid data, improve our processes. Such data is more usefully collected, made sense of, and acted upon locally. One of the truisms of learning is that those who have the ability to act on the results need to control the collection and interpretation of the data.

The role of traditional measurement systems is to provide data to senior management so that they can use it to make good decisions. Indeed this is the reasoning that underlies asking for proof that organizational learning is working in an organization. Top management is asking, 'Should we invest in organizational learning?'. However, the alternative use of measurement comes from a different way of thinking. It is about how you collect enough information about what you are doing to improve. Who gets the data is different and the purpose for collecting it is different.

The alternative way to view measurement is as a critical element in the learning process. Measurement data are very powerful if they are constructed by a group of people who meet together to determine what data they would need to collect to determine their effectiveness. They might decide on a set of measures and after collecting the data decide that they were not very useful and settle on a different set of data. It might require several attempts to obtain really useful data. Moreover what is useful would surely change over time. Assuming the group has developed useful data, they would need to meet together to make sense of the data and decide what actions to take. This is the learning use of measurement.

Meyer (1994), in discussing measurement for cross-functional teams, provides four guidelines:

1   The overarching purpose of a measurement system should

be to help a team, rather than top managers, gauge its progress.

2 A truly empowered team must play the lead role in designing its own measurement system.

3 Because a team is responsible for a value-delivery process that cuts across several functions (like product development, order fulfilment or customer service), it must create measures to track that process.

4 A team should adopt only a handful of measures. (p. 96)

It would be difficult to find a team or unit in an organization that did not have some measure they were keeping, schedule, costs, etc. It would be less difficult to find a team or unit that has measures designed to inform their own learning.

References

Bougon, M. G. (1983). 'Uncovering cognitive maps: the Self-Q Technique', in G. Morgan (ed.), *Beyond Method: Strategies for Social Research*. Beverly Hills CA: Sage.

Dixon, N. M. (1997). 'Action learning: More than just a task force' in M. Pedler (ed.), *Action Learning in Practice* (3rd edn.), pp. 329–38. Gower.

Kaplan, R. S. and Norton, D. P. (1996). 'Using the balanced scorecard as a strategic management system'. *Harvard Business Review*, January/February, 75–85.

Lee, Courtney and O'Keefe (1992). 'A system for organizational learning using cognitive maps'. *OMEGA International Journal of Management Science*, 1, 23–36.

March, J. G. and Olsen, H. P. (1976). *Ambiguity and Choice in Organizations*. Oslo, Norway: Universitetsforlaget.

Meyer, C. (1994). 'How the right measures help teams excel'. *Harvard Business Review*, May/June, 95–103.

Senge, P. M. (1990). *The Fifth Discipline*. New York: Doubleday.

Weick, K. E. and Bougon, M. G. (1986). 'Organizations as cognitive maps', in H. P. Sims and D. A. Gioia, *The thinking organization*, pp. 102–135. San Francisco: Jossey-Bass.

8 Developing managers for organizational learning*

Traditionally, management development programmes have taken participants away from work to learn from management experts. The experts or their surrogates stand in front of the class, sometimes electronically and sometimes in person, and explain to managers what they need to know in order to be successful and effective.

This way of developing managers is in contradiction to the concepts of organizational learning. Organizations are, on the one hand, encouraging managers to 'think for yourselves', and 'find new answers' while offering management development programmes that provide ready-made answers such as, 'Transformational leadership will solve these problems', 'You need to form self-managed teams', 'Here is the way to resolve conflict'. Management development classrooms are not neutral environments in which only content is learned; managers in classroom situations also learn the lessons of the context. For example, in traditional management development programmes managers

* This chapter is adapted from an article first published in *Human Resource Management Review,* **3** (3) (1993) 243–54.

learn to trust the solutions of experts rather than their own, to accept rather than question what those in authority say, and to withhold any serious problems they see with what they are learning. This process unintentionally mirrors the very relationship between managers and employees from which organizations are attempting to extricate themselves through organizational learning; that is, a relationship in which the manager is the one responsible, makes the decisions, has the most knowledge and does the most talking.

To be congruent with the fundamental assumptions of organizational learning, management development programmes would have to change substantially.

- As learning and work become synonymous learning *would need to come out of the classroom* and into spaces where work is being conducted.
- Learning, which has traditionally meant the comprehension of existing knowledge, would need also to include *creating new knowledge*.
- Learning, which has for so long been regarded as an individual activity, would need to be viewed as a *community* or collective activity.

Before turning to specific changes that need to be made in management development programmes in order to make them congruent with organizational learning, it may be helpful to review how I am using the term 'development'. In Chapter 2 I used Kegan's (1982) definition of development as the 'active process of increasingly organizing the relationship of the self to the environment. The relationship gets better organized by increasing differentiations of the self from the environment and thus by increasing integrations of the environment' (p. 114). In an organizational context the 'environment' includes such things as co-workers, job-related tasks, organizational strategy and top management of the organization. An example of development in this context might be a manager redefining his or her role in relation to subordinates, perhaps moving from the role of supervisor to that of coach, or from boss to team member.

In this example, however, development is not the change in behaviour, rather it is the internal reorganization of self in relationship to the subordinates that mediates the supervisor's behaviour.

Learning is differentiated from development, in that learning involves new techniques to function more effectively in an existing framework, whereas development is the movement from one framework to another. One of the consistent miscalculations made in management development programmes is the attempt to teach managers techniques for functioning that are inconsistent with the managers' existing frameworks. The result of that attempt is that managers often exhibit the new behaviour once or twice in the workplace and then revert to their former behaviour because the new technique 'doesn't work' or 'feels awkward'. This 'transfer problem' is most often blamed on lack of support from the immediate supervisor or on a culture that is at cross purposes with the new learning (Broad and Newstrom, 1992). It is, however, equally likely that the new behaviour does not fit the way that the managers have organized who they are in relationship to their environment. Learning, then, is about making sense of the world through an existing frame. Development is about a change in the frame itself.

Organizations can and do limit the development of individuals in many ways, for example, by preventing people from taking on challenging tasks, by establishing norms that make objects of people, by expecting individuals to act in ways that do not make sense to them. Likewise, organizations are themselves shaped and influenced by the developmental level of the individuals who comprise them. For example, individuals who see the world as dichotomous cannot create an organization capable of dealing with ambiguity. There is an interaction between the development of individuals and organizations that is both the hope and the difficulty of organizational change. The paradox is that an organization cannot change significantly unless the individuals who live in it themselves make significant change; however, those individuals are limited in their development by the system in which they function.

Four fundamental changes are suggested here that would

serve to make management development programmes more congruent with organizational learning. They are:

1   Situating learning in real work.
2   Defining a less central role for experts.
3   Spaced rather than compressed time frames.
4   Learning in community rather than individually.

Situating learning in real work

Sanford (1981) says that development occurs primarily in response to the challenges of life. It may be possible for managers to become more proficient at technical skills in a 'time away from work' setting, but development occurs in context. Management development cannot occur in the abstract, away from the issues and challenges of managing the organization, because those challenges provide the data and dissonance upon which the reorganization of self is based; they are the grist of the change. Even the more experiential forms of classroom training, such as case studies or role plays, cannot provide the level of reality that is needed for development. In such hypothetical activities the individual is not compelled to experience the frustration of failing at something he or she truly cares about, nor the deep concern that others will suffer for one's mistakes, nor experience the satisfaction of completion, nor the often overwhelming complexity of decisions. Development occurs when managers attempt to deal with real problems about which they care deeply so that their intellect, beliefs and emotions are all engaged. Revans (1983), the father of action learning, has said 'There can be no learning without action and no (sober and deliberate) action without learning' (p. 54).

However, facing real problems is not sufficient for development to occur. Huxley (1972) said 'Experience is not what happens to you, it's what you do with what happens to you'. There must also be the *intention* of learning from the experience. Kegan's (1982) definition quoted earlier suggests an *'active process* of increasingly organizing the relationship of the self to the environment'. Action must be accompanied by reflection on action and moreover on the outcomes of those actions. It is through reflection that the reorganization of self is accomplished. Reflection is most effective when it involves others who can provide perspective, that is, a view from outside the manager's current frame.

Situating learning in the workplace does not preclude managers coming together, but it does alter their reason for being together. The purpose is not to learn from an expert, or even to learn from each others' successes, but to reflect together on their own actions.

Defining a less central role for experts

Many traditional management development programmes incorporate action planning that might appear to satisfy the requirement for real work. In such programmes managers are encouraged to try out the principles they have learned back at their own work site: a 'theory-then-application' model. A reversal of that sequence is suggested here as being more compatible with organizational learning: a 'problem-then-theory+' model. To illustrate this model, assume a manager encounters a difficult problem in the workplace, perhaps a troubled relationship with a superior or frustration that the quality implementation has plateaued. Being apprised of the problem, a management development specialist or peers may be able to identify theory and principles that can inform the manager's understanding of the situation. The sequence, however, is 'problem-then-theory', not 'theory-then-application'.

The reversal is significant in that it echoes the new way organizations are attempting to deal with their problems. We are ending an era in which organizations sought *answers* from experts, whether the expert came in the form of the latest management book, an esteemed conference speaker, a famous consultant or the sacrosanct words of the training manual.

Organizational learning is not about seeking answers from experts. It is about collecting valid information from a variety of sources so that the information can be considered in terms of the local context and subjected to the reasoning of the minds of the stakeholders. Within the framework of organizational learning, experts are heard and their opinions considered, but organizational members do not relinquish their responsibility for critically reflecting on the information for themselves. Experts are needed and valued within the framework of organizational learning, but their role is less central to understanding than in the past. We are at the very beginning of an era in organizations in which the resolution of difficult issues is found in the reasoning and learning capability of organizational members.

Theory or expert opinion becomes one input among many that might inform the reasoning of a manager who is dealing with a difficult issue. The 'plus' in the problem-then-theory+ model includes one's peers, who may be able to help the manager examine his or her assumptions related to the problem and thereby see the problem in a new light; data that results from action; customers who provide yet another perspective; and other stakeholders who can lend additional perspective and data to the understanding.

The theory-then-apply model assumes that management development professionals are able to predict what issues managers are going to face and thus are able to supply, in advance, theory that will address those issues. The problem-then-theory+ model asserts that in a changing world it is difficult to predict what issues managers will be facing, but that for most real-world problems there are one or more theoretical frameworks that may be useful as one source of input for thinking through the problem.

Spaced rather than compressed time frames

Management development programmes have typically been provided within a compressed time format, that is a programme that may last three days or two weeks. Compressed schedules facilitate travel and minimize time away from work; they allow managers to 'get it over with' and 'get back to work'. The problem with compressed schedules for management development is that they do not result in development.

Development occurs over time. Time is needed to act, to see the results of one's action, to talk with others, to gain perspective, to review theory that might inform one's thinking, to act again, to reflect again, to let go of old ideas, to try anew. The rhythm of development matches the rhythm of the workplace, where challenges also occur over time; problems are exacerbated, get better, decline in importance, then resurface, are confounded with other issues, and are sometimes resolved through no action of our own. Development occurs through the challenges of real work; thus the schedule of a management development programme must correspond to the schedule of the work world. That means a management development programme may need to be spaced out over six months or a year.

If development is thought of as time away from work then a management development programme that lasts six months or a year is unreasonable. If, however, development is not separate from work but is accomplished through work with programme meetings that are spaced out over that period, then the programme is both more palatable and more effective.

Many traditional management development programmes include a kind of follow-up activity that consists of either bringing participants back together to see what they have accomplished or a phone call or survey to check on their progress. Neither of these activities is in the spirit of spaced learning. With spaced learning periodic meetings are a part of the learning, not a way to determine if learning occurred or to report on its results.

Learning in community rather than individually

Organizational learning requires individuals to think for themselves and to use their own reasoning in the service of the organization. For organizational learning to work, individuals' reasoning must be sound. However, as discussed in Chapter 2, the soundness of individual reasoning is often questionable. The tendency to look for evidence that supports an initial view, to give greater weight to more recent events and to fail to check out the inferences made from incomplete data are a few of the many ways individuals inhibit and limit their own learning.

The way individuals are able to correct for those human tendencies and thereby increase the robustness of their understanding is to test their conclusions against data. When the issues under consideration relate to the physical world, individuals can measure and count to obtain objective data. Unfortunately most of the critical issues managers face are matters of interpretation not fact; for example, what strategy to implement to increase market share, or which person would function most effectively as CEO. In equivocal situations, the validity of ideas must be tested, not by facts, but against the reasoning of others. When individuals lay out their conclusions, their evidence, and their reasoning, others can confirm it or point to the flaws they perceive. Individuals need others to see what they have reasoned incorrectly and what they are themselves blind to. Thus, much of the learning that is critical to organizations requires others to accomplish it – it is learning that necessitates collaboration.

Collaboration involves two factors, confrontation and cooperation. Collaborative learning occurs when conclusions are confronted – but only when that confrontation is in the spirit of increased understanding rather than 'winning'. Collaborative learning is not a perfect solution to the fallacies of human reasoning, but the results are significantly better than individualistic learning efforts designed into most management development programmes.

One explanation for this phenomenon lies in the positive

effects of dissonance. When participants in an interaction are confronted by a position which they see as sound, yet realize conflicts with their own position, which they also believe to be sound, they experience cognitive dissonance. In an effort to reduce the dissonance, participants search for additional information to support their position and also seek to understand the opposing position, data and supporting rationale. They use the skills of critical analysis and inductive and deductive reasoning to develop, clarify, expand and elaborate their thinking about the issues being considered. As a result of this reflection participants in the interaction reconstruct their meaning, incorporating new information or reframe the way they view an issue (Johnson and Johnson, 1989, pp. 91–2; Tetlock and Kim, 1987).

Thus far two important reasons for a focus on collective learning have been suggested: the help others can offer in validating equivocal ideas, and the benefit of dissonance for the development of increased understanding. There is yet a third argument for collective learning. When managers develop they move from their existing frame to a new and more differentiated frame. The period of transition that occurs as the manager lets go of his or her current way of organizing the world and constructs a new, more differentiated frame is a time of confusion and loss. The manager must come to recognize that the way he or she has been functioning is inadequate and the normal result is to doubt one's own competence. At the same time managers may experience a new sense of hope and promise for the future, the exhilaration that comes with insight. In such a confusing time individuals need the support of others and the knowledge that others have similar experiences. The community of learners provides an environment that both initiates and supports development.

No guarantees

Management development is a gamble in two ways. First it is not possible to predict whether a development process will work for every manager. Some managers may not develop even when engaged in the best of programmes. Development is to some extent dependent upon readiness. A manager may have recently been through a period of transition with which he or she is still involved, others may be absorbed in personal issues and cannot afford additional disruption in their lives, still others may be so well satisfied with their situation that little dissonance is generated. Lack of movement does not mean a manager cannot or will not develop, it may only mean that now is not the right time.

The second gamble is that there are no guarantees about the direction in which a manager may develop. Development as the reorganization of the self in relation to the world is unique to each individual. One manager may come to see that he has been putting too much energy into work or has been taken advantage of by the organization. Another individual may come to see that the goals of the organization do not represent her values or that the organization's policies are detrimental to the community. It is not possible to say to managers 'Think critically about these issues but not about certain other issues' or 'Examine your own assumptions to see how you may be part of the problem but do not question the assumptions of the organization'. There is an emancipation component of development. An organization that promotes the development of its managers must be open to its own development.

Illustrations of management development programmes

To facilitate organizational learning, four fundamental changes in the way management development is designed have been suggested:

1 Situating learning in real work.
2 Defining a less central role for experts.
3 Spaced rather than compressed time frames.
4 Learning in community rather than individually.

Four examples of management development programmes that meet many, if not all four, changes are briefly described.

Northern Telecom: global leadership forum

This programme is designed for Northern Telecom's top 150 managers. Managers participate in the programme in addition to accomplishing their regular jobs, spending up to one third of their time on the programme during the seven-month period that the programme lasts.

There are two objectives for the programme:

1 To resolve a pressing business issue.
2 Individual learning, which includes self-knowledge, learning about global market issues, and global teamwork.

Each class has 24 managers who are divided into four teams of six people. The teams are made up of individuals from different functional areas. Each team has an executive sponsor at the corporate level. The teams work on problems which have been identified by senior-level executives, for example, how to do low-cost production in digital switching, or how to manage human resources on a global basis. It is important that the project selected for the team is one that is outside the team members' area of expertise.

The programme begins with six days in the USA. During this period the teams are formed and participants work on team building as well as receiving considerable feedback from instruments that have been completed by subordinates and peers prior to coming to the programme. During this time the teams also define their plan to gather information on the problem.

During the next months the teams go all over the world to benchmark and collect data. They may also assign their staff to help them as well as negotiating with others to help. At midcourse all the teams come together for four days in Europe. Here the teams review their progress but also participate in seminars on cross-cultural issues.

The teams continue working on the project for the next few months. At the end of seven months the teams come together again for two days. The Chairman of Northern Telecom and the Vice-Presidents are present to hear the solutions the teams have developed. Each team has half a day to present. The executive group listens to the presentations and makes a go/no go decision on each.

Executive Education, San Diego State University

Each participant in this University Executive programme has a high-level sponsor in his or her home organization who has identified a project the participant is to work on during the programme. As the focus of the programme is strategy, many of the projects are planning tasks, although some include implementation as well. Participants are each assigned from one to three interns from the university to assist them with their projects.

The programme lasts fourteen weeks and includes ten evenings, with some full days interspersed. Participants meet in teams to help each other with the problems they are addressing. In addition to the team meetings, university faculties make presentations on relevant topics, such as change, finance and human resources. For each topic there are also two CEOs who talk about the concepts the faculty presents in relation to their own organization.

Volvo Truck Management (VTM) programme

The expected results of the VTM programme are:

- Expanded self-insight and leadership development.
- Solutions to several company-wide problems.
- An evolving corporate culture which is better able to meet the emerging business opportunities of the ever-changing world.

The VTM programme is twenty-five days in length spread over an eight-month period. The programme is held in four different countries, for one week every two months. Twenty-five participants are selected from different divisions and countries to represent the multinational and multicultural character of Volvo Truck. Participants are nominated by the management teams in the different divisions.

Headquarters and different divisions propose projects with the final selection of projects being made by the programme advisory board. Criteria for selection of the projects include that a project must:

- be a global project that has regional implications
- be of strategic importance
- offer possibilities for risk taking
- have a quantifiable payoff
- be at a general management level.

In the programme, participants work in teams of five on problems which fall in areas outside of their present functional responsibilities. Each team analyses its problem and may redefine it if necessary in order to come up with workable solutions that will satisfy the project host, the person who owns the problem.

During the week-long residencies about half of the time is reserved for project work and the other half for seminars. Experts both from inside and outside Volvo serve as seminar leaders. A facilitator is assigned to each team to help the group work together as a team, to ensure that both the individuals and the team as a whole learn, and that the project hosts' needs are met.

The programme results not only meet the stated goals, but the programme launches a dialogue between participants and top management about the strategic issues of Volvo Truck.

Center for Creative Leadership: LeaderLab®
The goal of LeaderLab® is to help participants take more effective action in leadership situations. Participants must be

nominated to participate and are selected with an eye for having diversity in the class.

As pre-work to the programme, participants complete numerous self-assessment and 360° feedback instruments as well as completing an audit of their current work situation. To explain, 360° feedback occurs when peers, subordinates and the participant's boss all respond to questionnaires about the participant's behaviour. Prior to attending the first meeting, each participant is contacted by a process advisor who will serve as his or her personal coach over the six months of the programme (Young and Dixon, 1996).

The programme begins with six days at the Center for Creative Leadership, during which participants receive personalized feedback on the instrumentation, develop strategies for effective action and set goals for themselves to be carried out in their back-home setting. Participants in the programme have change partners in the class with whom they process what they are learning from lectures and a number of non-traditional learning activities. Each participant keeps a learning journal which is used for reflection and to communicate with process advisors. Participants are asked to set up change partners in their home work site as well.

After their initial six days, participants return to their work for three months during which time they carry out the plan they have developed for taking more effective leadership action. Their process advisor talks with them monthly about how they are achieving the goals they have set.

After three months, participants return to the Center for four days, during which they debrief the three months of implementation and reassess their goals and strategies. During this time they again work with their process advisor and change partners.

Again participants return to their work to continue the implementation of their plan, often reworked over the four days at the Center. The programme ends after six months with an in-depth written summary of the experience and closure with the process advisor.

It is always a challenge for organizations to create congruence between new ways of thinking and the organization's support systems such as training, performance management, rewards and recognition, and selection. In this chapter I have focused on one aspect of training – management development. It is a particularly critical area, because in most organizations it is the mechanism through which the new behaviours are learned. If management development sends a mixed message about the new ways of thinking, it is not only confusing, it works against the change.

References

Broad, M. and Newstrom, J. (1992). *Transfer of Training: Action-Packed Strategies to Ensure High Payoff From Training Investment*. Reading MA: Addison-Wesley.

Huxley, A. (1972). 'Visionary experience', in J. White (ed.), *The Highest State of Consciousness*. New York: Archer.

Johnson, D. W. and Johnson, R. T. (1989). *Cooperation and Competition: Theory and Research*. Edina MN: Interaction Book Company.

Kegan, R. (1982). *The Evolving Self*. Cambridge MA: Harvard University Press.

Revans, R. W. (1983). *ABC of Action Learning*. Bromley, Kent: Chartwell-Bratt Ltd.

Sanford, N (1981). 'Notes toward a theory of personality development at 80', in J. R. Starde (ed.), *In Wisdom and Old Age*. Berkeley CA: Ross Books.

Tetlock, P. E. and Kim, J. I. (1987). 'Accountability and judgment processes in a personality prediction task'. *Journal of Personal and Social Psychology*, **57**, 700–9.

Young, D. P. and Dixon, N. M. (1996). *Helping Leaders Take Effective Action: A Program Evaluation*. Greensboro NC: Center for Creative Leadership.

9 The responsibilities of members in an organization that is learning*

Francis Bacon (1825) said, that knowledge is power. His actual words were *nam et ipsa scientia potestas est*, 'Knowledge itself is a power'. What makes organizational learning so powerful is that it is a fundamental change in what we believe about *who* has knowledge. Organizational learning proclaims that knowledge grows out of the ongoing experience of all organizational members; it is they who create and hold the organization's knowledge. That belief contrasts sharply with the more traditional belief that there are two classes within organizations, thinkers and doers. Organizational learning declares that doers are also thinkers; knowledge creators. When the source of knowledge shifts, so does the power. Where knowledge is, power is.

If organizational learning represents a fundamental shift in power, then we can no longer regard it as a management tool, or at least not *only* a management tool. With this shift it is clear that it is not only managers that need to be thinking about how

* This chapter is adapted from an article first published in *The Learning Organization*, vol. 5, Nov, 1998, pp. 161–67.

to make organizational learning happen or how to function differently – all members need to be considering their responsibilities and roles in such an organization.

This chapter then is directed to people at all levels as a way to begin a necessary dialogue about their responsibilities in an organization that is learning. However, in presenting these ideas, I am immediately faced with a language difficulty. We do not have a term in common usage that means everyone in the organization. The term 'employee', in its common usage, refers only to those people who are not in management positions, although we would all readily acknowledge that managers are also employed by organizations. To be easily understood I am obliged to say 'managers and employees', or 'people at all levels of the organization'. Our language, or lack of it in this case, reflects how pervasive this division of 'thinkers' and 'doers' is and how difficult it is for us to conceive of ourselves as a whole.

Throughout this book I have used the term 'organizational members' to refer to people at all levels of the organization. My use of the term is an attempt, through language, to integrate the organization; to be inclusive. The words that we use in talking about organizational learning are critical because our language influences the meaning we create, as well as being a reflection of that meaning. We create organizational learning by the way we talk about it; by the words we choose. '[L]anguage holds forth the historically developed dimensions of interests, the lines along which things will be distinguished' (Deetz, 1992). It is not insignificant that there is no term in common usage that includes everyone in the organization.

This chapter considers the responsibilities of organizational members without dividing those responsibilities into ones assigned to differing levels. The question, then, is what should organizational members mutually hold themselves accountable for if they are committed to the organization's learning?

The term 'responsibility' suggests a willingness to be held *accountable*; to be answerable for our actions. We often think in terms of being responsible *to* some person, for example, each level in the organization sees itself as being responsible *to* the next higher level. In terms of organizational learning, I am suggesting members also have responsibilities to the collective or the whole. Joint responsibility is present in many human systems: for example, we have responsibilities to a particular political party but also to the nation as a whole; we have responsibilities to a spouse but also to the family as a whole. This chapter addresses the responsibilities members have to the organization as a whole, not to the exclusion of others, but in addition to them. What does it mean to function as a member of an organization that is learning? How would members see themselves differently in an organization that is learning than in a more traditional organization? How would their expectations of themselves in relation to the whole be different?

Organizational learning offers us an enormous potential, if we take the opportunity it affords us, to think anew about how to 'be in' an organization; or even how to be an organization. And likewise its potential is substantially reduced if it is positioned as something one part of the organization wants another part to do – another 'management fad'. If it is perceived only as a way to accomplish greater productivity or a way to reduce the product development cycle, it will not live up to the possibilities it holds. Those are certainly not unworthy goals, but they are limited to doing what we have been doing; only better and faster of course. Organizational learning has the potential, if we choose to take advantage of it, to help us rethink what an organization is and what it means to work in an organizational setting.

Every new organizational idea that comes along, and I will put organizational learning temporarily in that category, is necessarily based on assumptions about such things as authority, human nature, and the type of knowledge that is valued. These assumptions both limit and define the ends which the idea can serve. We could analyse any current or past organizational idea to reveal the assumptions of its creators or implementers. As an example, cross-functional teams, which have become increasingly prevalent in organizations, are based on assumptions drawn from systems theory, e.g. that organizations are made up of interdependent subsystems which must work in concert to achieve a system goal; and that changing any part of the system requires concomitant changes in other parts – thus cross-functional teams recognize the interdependence within organizations and are an effective means to address it.

To carry the contrast further, the assumptions underlying the use of cross-functional teams differ greatly from those of Management By Objectives (MBO), for example, which, based on a more mechanistic conception of organizations, presumes that if each part of the organization performs competently and efficiently, the organization as a whole will necessarily function more effectively. The goal of MBO is control and predictability. We would not expect MBO to assist in developing a more flexible and responsive system, just as we would not expect cross-functional teams to provide greater control and predictability; each is based on a different way of thinking about organizations and thus responds to differing perceptions of need. I'm not suggesting that organizational members typically sit down over coffee and say to each other 'Given our growing belief in systems theory we ought to have multi-functional teams'. But I am suggesting that the mental models we hold about organizations impact the kinds of ideas we introduce into our organizations. There is a clear link between the assumptions on which such ideas are based and the outcomes they are able to bring about, even though those assumptions are often implicit rather than explicit.

The assumptions on which organizational learning is based are articulated throughout this book. They are summarized here:

1   Organizational members learn in the act of doing their work; learning and work are intertwined.
2   Organizational learning is not primarily about obtaining 'correct information', rather it is fundamentally about people 'making sense' of the experience they have.
3   We all need the perspective of others to help us see what we are blind to in our own experience.
4   In order for learning to occur, individuals and teams need

to be able to act upon what they have learned locally through their own experience.

5 What an organization 'knows' is distributed across its members.

6 An organization, as a collective, has the capability to understand the difficult issues it faces.

7 Organizations are changeable and malleable; through the ongoing organizational dialogue members can alter the organization and influence the purposes it serves.

Given these assumptions, organizational learning has the potential, over time, to change an organization's way of doing business internally. As those who are well into the implementation of organizational learning can affirm, it creates a more egalitarian organization which shifts the distribution of power; it affects the purpose of the organization to be more inclusive; it develops a more collaborative culture. I view it as so powerful I have sometimes thought of it as 'unleashing a dragon' with power that is both awesome and frightening.

Five responsibilities that offer a new way of thinking

I have outlined five possible responsibilities that I think offer a new way to begin thinking about how to 'be in' an organization. Some may be perceived as expecting too much of organizational members and some will be thought of as too idealistic. Some might be welcomed by those in positions of management, while others may be seen as giving too much ascendancy to people who are not in positions of authority. The responsibilities of the members in an organization that is learning, if it is to be different than in a traditional organization, will certainly evolve over time as members act out the roles they take on.

Actively engage in organizational dialogue that continually examines the worth of the organization's purpose

Organizational learning is often heralded as a *means* an organization can use to reach a desired end, such as maintaining a competitive edge or obtaining a larger share of market. I support the concept that organizational learning can be an effective means to reach such organizational goals. I also want to suggest that organizational learning is also about *ends* and that both means and ends are the subject of learning. This should not surprise us, because as individuals all of us have, at some time, experienced going to school or taking a new position in order to reach a goal we have set for ourselves, only to discover that the goal we were aiming for has itself altered in the process of our learning. As our understanding grew we learned that our goal was too limited or that there was a more satisfying goal that we preferred. For organizations as well, collective learning can result in a redefinition of the collective goal. As organizational members think together about the work they are doing (e.g. challenging each other's assumptions, bringing in diverse perspectives) it is likely that the organization's purpose will be questioned and sometimes enlarged or altered.

I suggest that not only does a redefinition of the end occur as a side-effect, but should also occur as an objective of organizational learning. I go so far as to say it is a responsibility of organizational members to engage in the continual re-examination of their organization's purpose. Any human system is in jeopardy when members view themselves as responsible only for the means, leaving it to others to determine the goal toward which the means are enacted. Means and ends are inexorably linked and need to be continually re-examined and challenged. One of the dangers we are always susceptible to is allowing means to become ends. The familiar story of the executive who wants to provide his family with a good life and so works hard to succeed in the company is apocryphal. Over time, he finds himself working harder and harder in the company, but in order to succeed in the company, he may begin to neglect his family. The means have become the end without him even recognizing that it has happened. Families are not the only system in which such paradoxes occur. Hospitals, for example, are notorious for allowing the need for order and regulation to become the ends rather than the means of enabling patients to gain their health back. Organizational members cannot absolve themselves of the responsibility of insuring that the goal toward which they are working is worthy and that the means has not become confused with the ends.

Organizational members' responsibility is to be cognizant of the goal (the ends) which their work serves and when, through their learning, they see ways in which the goal is limited or questionable, to engage in public dialogue to challenge or question it. By 'public' dialogue I mean making their conclusions and their reasoning 'accessible' to others in the organization. 'Public' is the opposite of talking privately to a few friends about such issues. It means saying in a public forum (staff meeting, team meeting, intra-net, town hall etc.) 'Here is a concern I have, what do others think about it?' It may mean saying it more than once. It may also mean *creating* public forums that provide the opportunity for bringing multiple perspectives to bear on the issue of ends (e.g. dialogue groups, intra-net discussion groups, book review groups, informal lunch meetings).

Bring the *best available knowledge* to bear on organizational issues

This responsibility is about surfacing information that is critical to addressing organizational issues. It may mean sending bad news up the hierarchy, making sure a group is included in a meeting because they have vital information, or practising 'open book management'. If organizational members have information that is critical to addressing an organizational issue and choose to withhold that information, they are colluding in a way that makes them jointly responsible for the outcome. I am not talking about whistle blowing, but about everyday courage to say what needs to be said. It is a matter of living out Argyris' governing variable of providing 'valid information'.

It is a very difficult responsibility to meet. Most of us do not deliberately lie, but we feel it is okay to 'just not say anything'. Block (1987) talks about it as caution versus courage. This responsibility requires members '. . . to confront an issue when others are acting as if there is no issue; to say that a meeting is not going well when everyone else seems totally satisfied. This is not a bells and whistles kind of courage . . . Organizational courage is required when the sides are somewhat murky, when the issue in and of itself is less than monumental, and when we feel that top management is in fact not on our side' (p.15).

There are many rationalizations that we use to excuse ourselves from bringing the best available knowledge to bear on organizational issues: 'They don't want to hear it.' 'You just don't challenge people who are in power.' 'That would be a career limiting statement.' 'I'm just trying to protect my people.' 'They would not understand the complexities of this problem.' 'There's no need to get people upset until we have more information.' 'It's not my responsibility, I just work here.' These rationalizations are disputed by this statement of responsibility. This responsibility is a challenge to top management no less than a challenge to the line; there is a shared responsibility to bring the best available knowledge to bear on any organizational issue. Organizational members cannot act in the best interest of the organization, nor in their own best interest without complete and valid information. And certainly learning is hampered when knowledge is withheld.

There are certainly ways to assist organizational members in living up to this responsibility. There are communication skills that organizational members can develop (for example, Argyris' Model II skills outlined in Chapter 2), that help to frame information in accurate but non-threatening ways. There are conditions or environments that organizational members can enact (such as those suggested in Chapter 5) that make both giving and receiving information more likely. All are helpful but none addresses the central issue, which is the question of whether organizational members view this as a mutual responsibility.

Function as a *co-participant* in the creation, maintenance and transformation of organizational realities

Each of us, by our language and our actions (both tacit and explicit), continually creates the reality we function within. Block (1987) says, 'Autonomy is the attitude that my actions are my own choices and the organization I am a part of is in many ways my own creation' (p.15).

In order to function as a co-participant, members would first have to believe that they have a right to co-create and co-transform the organizational realities. This would be a big change for many organizational members who more commonly see themselves as players in someone else's game, e.g. the CEO, the executive team, or the board. Organizational members often view themselves as having only two choices, comply or leave. There is a third choice that is voiced in the statement of this responsibility, to acknowledge that by colluding through their silence or their agreement with others, they have helped to create the organization as it exists, and to accept the challenge to co-create it in a form that is more satisfying.

Secondly, organizational members would have to believe it is possible for the organization to change. Organizational members who have functioned within a bureaucratic framework for many years often become so resigned to the reality they experience that they believe 'this is just the way organizations are', and no longer recognize that all organization forms are a product of the human mind and can therefore also be altered by human minds.

If members took this responsibility of co-participant seriously and believed the organization could change, then they would say to themselves, 'Do I approve of the culture and norms of this organization I work within? Is this the kind of organization I value?' If the answer was 'yes', they could consider how to sustain and build on the reality they had created. If the answer was 'no', they would engage in a 'public' discussion that would help to define a more acceptable culture or norms.

Willingly *share what each knows* with colleagues and create forums and systems to accomplish it

This responsibility involves each team or individual making what they have learned available to others; lateral communication. But it is about more than just sending an e-mail to a list serve or copying others on a memo. It means taking an *active* role in understanding what others know that would be helpful to one's own unit and about taking an active role in identifying the information one's own unit has that others could use and then creating joint meetings, databases and information exchanges that meet those needs. It means assuming the responsibility for sharing knowledge.

This responsibility raises the troublesome issue of who owns what organizational members know. The question is not so difficult if we are talking about patents or inventions; there the answer is clear cut and may even be written into the employment contract. The question is more difficult when, for example, a team has found a way to reduce cost on materials. Is the team responsible for sharing that information with other teams? If a salesperson has figured out a way to bundle three products so that they sell twice as much, is that something she can just use for her own advantage or does that knowledge belong to all of the salespeople in the firm? Constant, Kiesler and Sproull (1994) found in their studies that organizational members view tangible information, such as a computer program or a written document, as belonging to the organization; but that they view intangible information, such as the ability to fix a software bug or their learned experience, as a part of themselves. This view makes sharing information a much more personal issue, one that requires a personal commitment. Yet because sharing is by definition mutual it is not a responsibility that any one member can accept without the concurrence of others.

This sharing responsibility then is not easily endorsed. It requires considerable deliberation among organizational members. It is surely predicated on a sense of 'we' rather than 'I' or 'them'. And the sense of 'we' is influenced by such things as how organizational members are rewarded, the extent to which organizational policy places units in competition with each other for scarce resources, and employment practices that encourage investment in self rather than investment in the organization.

Actively *learn from experience* every day to develop as a responsible, participating member of the organization

This responsibility is more than just 'keeping up to date' in one's technical specialty, although that is an important responsibility in its own right. It is the responsibility to continually:

1   Experiment (try new ways to do things).
2   Reflect on what has happened as a result of individual or team action.
3   Reflect with others on the action of the whole system in order to learn how to make it function better.

It means having a 'learning' attitude about work. It is an active rather than a passive role; being engaged intellectually rather than just complying.

There are many ways to do this; some are illustrated in the stories of Chaparral Steel and Johnsonville Foods in Chapter 4 and some are outlined in Chapter 6. Ideas there range from teams holding lessons learned meetings to actively tracking results. Here I want to focus less on *how* to learn from experience, and more on the idea that it is a *responsibility* of organizational members; their willingness to participate in such meetings and even to call for such meetings.

Again this responsibility applies as much to management as to non-management organizational members. I am concerned that too often management has held the attitude that 'we (management) are ready to take on new ideas, it is only getting others "on board" that is difficult'. Management teams and individual managers also need to be responsible for learning from their own experience. They need to have lessons learned meetings in which they ask themselves, 'How well did we do that? What can we learn from how we did this, not about others, but about ourselves? What might we do differently next time? How do we measure our performance?'

The commitment to learning needs to be both to individual learning and to collective learning. The commitment to individual learning is easier to support, because we can take any learning we gain from our experience with us if we leave the organization. The commitment to collective learning is more problematic because it means we make an investment in the whole. And we are aware that we may not get that investment back, particularly in a time when organizations view downsizing as a justifiable way to reduce costs for the short run. Being willing to invest in collective learning is clearly a long-term investment on the part of organizational members. For it to work there also has to be a long-term investment in organizational members on the part of the organization.

Sharing in the responsibility for the *governance* of the organization

All of these responsibilities pertain to organizational members sharing more fully in the governance of the organization. Governance is about making decisions in the name of the organization. In most organizations decision making is firmly rooted in the hierarchical chain, although we increasingly see the hierarchy giving up some of its decision-making privilege to teams or individuals. Although it is widely acknowledged that such teams or individuals are given decision-making authority at the discretion of the hierarchy, in actuality the converse is also true. That is, who can legitimately make decisions in the name of the organization, is *granted* by those who are governed.

This idea is perhaps easier to grasp if we examine examples of governance that occur outside of corporate boundaries. We grant the police governance authority in certain areas, but we would not countenance their authority in other areas. If, for example, a police officer were to pull us over for wearing inappropriate clothing, like a sweater instead of a suit, we would not tolerate their authority. We would say, 'You have no right to specify what clothing I wear'. We give legislators governance authority in certain areas, but tell them to stay out of others. Governance is granted by the governed. It works only because the governed *recognize* the legitimization of the claim made by those in authority.

Likewise within organizations. Most of us would accept that our bosses can specify dress code, what tasks we are to do, what hours we are to maintain etc. If, however, our boss were to attempt to tell us how many children we should have or which church we should go to, we might see that as outside the range of the legitimate authority. We grant the organization the right to govern us in some areas but not in others. We may not even recognize that we have made such a tacit agreement until we are able to see the situation through the eyes of another culture or time.

If, as I am suggesting, top management governs with the consent of organizational members, then important questions have to be asked. Do we as organizational members consent to the layoff of 5000 of our members? Do we consent to paying labour in Mexico 39 cents an hour? Do we consent to employing children in factories in Third World countries? Do we consent to pumping as much poisonous gas into the environment as we can legally get away with?

I suggest that, as organizational members, we have a role in governance of the organization, whether or not we choose to acknowledge that role. In this responsibility statement, I am suggesting we are a part of the governance structure and we need to take that responsibility seriously.

How would we do that? By giving voice to our concerns. By demanding open access to information. By forming committees or task forces to oversee issues that we see as critical. By demanding the replacement of decision makers who make decisions that we see as wrong.

Preparing organizational members for their responsibilities

If, as suggested, organizational members have responsibilities beyond compliance, then they should be about the task of considering what those responsibilities are and how to carry them out. Organizational members should not be relegated to being the recipients of the thinking of others about these important issues (whether it is my ideas that I have put forth above or the CEO's ideas in a company), but they should be the originators and discussants of such ideas. Organizational members should be full participants in the dialogue about the responsibilities they are to assume.

To contemplate such ideas, organizational members will need space and time for doing so. They will need vehicles through which to make public their ideas and ways to hear and reflect on conflicting perspectives. It is a significant shift in thinking that I am suggesting here. Management cannot *give* or grant to organizational members a shift in thinking. Organizational members must themselves shift their thinking through dialogue with each other. Management's role is not insignificant in this process, their thinking must also shift – but management cannot do the thinking work of others.

In our current organizations there are few such forums that facilitate the kind of in-depth dialogue that is necessary. Moreover, in our organizational culture as a whole, there are few vehicles that either acknowledge the need for such a dialogue or provide access to the means to engage in such a dialogue. There are no journals directed to organizational members. The journals that deal with issues of organizational change, learning, culture, strategy etc. are directed to managers or executives. Likewise, organizations offer programmes for managers to teach them about these same issues, while few, if any, such programmes exist for organizational members. It is the same in universities; courses about organizational issues are targeted at managers or those who aspire to management. Universities offer organizational members only courses in how to do their technical work more effectively, but not what it means to be an effective and responsible organizational member.

In writing this book I recognize that I am as much a part of the problem as are others. This book, like most, will be marketed to and purchased primarily by managers. Moreover, when I work with organizations in a consulting capacity, it is with management that I work. They are (I hear myself and others say) the ones who are willing to pay the consulting fees. This selective attention reveals our tacit assumptions, as a culture, that those who are responsible for the system, and more importantly who are responsible for *changing* the system, are those who are in management roles.

Over the next few years, as organizations enact their growing understanding that organizational knowledge resides within organizational members, these issues of responsibility will require careful and thoughtful attention. We do not know much about how to be an effective member of an organization that is learning. We only know how to be a member of a bureaucracy with its responsibilities spelled out by the reporting relationships of the hierarchy. We are so embedded in this model, that it is extremely difficult for us to think about new kinds of organization. As soon as we start down that road we are stopped by the roadblock of *what is*. Schein (1989) says: 'Our thinking about these matters is hampered by one major, deeply embedded cultural assumption so taken for granted that it is difficult even to articulate. This is the assumption that all organizations are fundamentally hierarchical in nature, and that the management process is fundamentally hierarchical. We need new models, but we may have difficulty inventing them because of the automatic tendency to think hierarchically' (p. 63). Organizational learning is an invitation to invent these new models; but we will have to invent them together. It is time to begin the dialogue.

References

Bacon, F. in B. Montagu (ed.) (1825). *The Works of Francis Bacon, Lord Chancellor of England*. London: William Pickering.

Block, P. (1987). *The Empowered Manager: Positive Political Skills at Work*. San Francisco: Jossey-Bass Inc.

Constant, D., Kiesler, S., Sproull, L. (1994). 'What's mine is ours, or is it? A study of attitudes about information sharing'. *Information Systems Research* **5** (4), 400–421.

Deetz, S. A. (1992). *Democracy in an Age of Corporate Colonization*. State University of New York Press.

Schein, E. (1989). 'Reassessing the "Divine Rights" of Managers.' *Sloan Management Review*, Winter, 63–68.

Zuboff, S. (1982). 'New worlds of computer-mediated work'. *Harvard Business Review*, September/October.

10 Defining a culture that supports learning

Organizational culture is the set of collective meaning structures that organizational members use to interpret the nature of their world and themselves in relation to it. They are assumptions that are so fundamental that they are for the most part tacit. They are not questioned unless attention is drawn to them by circumstances which shake 'what we thought we knew' or by 'externals' whose taken-for-granted assumptions so differ from the organization's that the organization's assumptions are noteworthy to the 'externals'.

That all members hold collective meaning structures in common implies that they are learned. There are at least two sources from which these assumptions are learned. One is the larger culture in which the organization is embedded, that is the industry, nation or hemisphere. For example, Bellah et al. (1985) have researched the way that individualism, which has been a basic assumption in the US since its colonial days, has affected its culture; individualism is a cornerstone of the US legal system, personal relationships, schooling, and even religious practices. People learn their assumptions about individualism through their daily interaction with others who are a part of that society, and having learned the assumptions reinforce them in others through their own actions. Thus individuals are both recipients of and creators of the culture. Individuals bring their assumptions into their organizations, shaping organizations to match the societal assumptions, and individualism is a basic assumption embedded in most US organizations. This assumption is particularly evident when a US organization attempts to initiate a team strategy, only to find that most of its functions, pay, promotion, reporting and training are designed to support individualism rather than teams.

Zuboff (1982) provides a time-related illustration of the way societal assumptions may affect an organization.

One day, in the 1860s, the owner of a textile mill in Lowell, Massachusetts posted a new set of work rules. In the morning, all weavers were to enter the plant at the same time, after which the factory gates would be locked until the close of the work day. By today's standards this demand that they arrive at the same time seems benign. Today's workers take for granted both the division of the day into hours of work and nonwork and the notion that everyone should abide by a similar schedule. But in the 1860s the weavers were outraged by the idea that an employer had the right to dictate the hours of labor. They said it was a 'system of slavery,' and went on strike. Eventually, the owner left the factory gates open and withdrew his demands. Several years later, the owner again insisted on collective work hours. As the older form of work organization was disappearing from other plants as well, the weavers could no longer protest. (p. 142)

In addition to widely shared societal basic assumptions, there are cultural assumptions which are learned and held within specific organizations. For example, an organization may be action-oriented, allocating little time for either planning or reflection. The cultural norm is reflected in conversations by phrases such as, 'It's better to do something than nothing' and 'We're not going to get anywhere just sitting around talking about it, let's do something'. In a different organization the culture may be more concerned with being 'right' than with acting. The conversation reflects this: 'Let's take our time to think this through'; 'Don't go off half-cocked'. To some extent people are likely to self-select themselves into an organization that is compatible with their own assumptions; but there is also a great deal of cultural learning that occurs after a new member has joined an organization. Some of that learning is deliberate, being offered through orientation or other training programmes, but most of it occurs through the daily interactions the new member has with others who hold such assumptions tacit. Much of the organization's culture is learned gradually, over time, and without the conscious intent of either the new or existing members.

Schein (1992) identifies three levels of organizational culture. He places assumptions at the base, regarding them as having the greatest impact on the organization and at the same time being the most difficult to decipher. Espoused values are the middle level. Values may be explicated in mission statements or policy documents, or may simply be evident in the conversation of organizational members, as in the quotes above. But, as Argyris et al. (1985) have argued so effectively, the values the organization espouses may in fact be in contradiction to its basic assumptions. Therefore, it is not possible to discern an organization's culture from an examination of its values.

The most visible and explicit parts of a culture are the artefacts (the top layer), which are such things as the architecture, the way space is allocated in the parking lot, the way organizational members dress and how they address each other. These and hundreds of other artefacts are observable, yet as Schein notes, are often misinterpreted in the absence of an understanding of the organization's basic assumptions. One difficulty in using the artefacts as indicators of culture lies in the fact that any interpretation of artefacts is made through the lens of the interpreter's own assumptions. A second difficulty is the multiple meanings any one artefact may have. For example, organizational members may dress formally because they maintain a formal relationship with each other or because they are responding to the expectations of their clients who are themselves formal. Schein holds that if an organizational culture is to be understood, the investigation must go beyond artefacts and espoused values and must examine the organization's basic assumptions.

There are six general areas of assumptions that Schein suggests examining to understand an organization's culture. They are:

1   *The nature of reality and truth*: How we can know if something is true or real? Is truth discovered empirically, through experience, or reached by agreement?
2   *The nature of time*: What is most important, the past, the present, or the future? Is time linear or circular? Do events develop over time, as in the development of an infant, or do we alter and control events to fit our time demands?
3   *The nature of space*: Is space shared or owned as in private property? What is the relationship of space to intimacy?
4   *The nature of human nature*: Are humans malleable or genetically fixed? Are individuals, by nature, self-motivated and curious or lazy and passive?
5   *The nature of human activity*: Are human beings a part of the environment or controllers and users of it?
6   *The nature of human relationships*: What level of responsibility do individuals have for others? Are human beings basically individualistic or group oriented? Are they competitive or cooperative? What is the proper role of authority in the lives of individuals? On what is authority based, law, morality, consensus?

The basic assumptions an organization embraces have an impact on every aspect of its functioning, the way it is structured, the goals it chooses, the strategies it employs to reach those goals, and certainly how it approaches learning. Some assumptions simply result in differing approaches to learning, while others have a fundamental impact on how well the organization is able to learn. In this chapter I have constructed a continuum for eight categories of assumptions in which I have placed the view most conducive to organizational learning on the right and the view which, from my perspective, is less favourable, on the left. For each end of the continuum I have described the learning approach that corresponds to that view. I have addressed those suggested by Schein which seem most related to learning and have added two that Schein does not consider.

Many of the assumptions outlined here were introduced earlier in other forms. I repeat them here in brief to place them within the context of organizational culture.

The nature of reality and truth

The assumptions that serve as poles of this continuum (see Figure 10.1) are the social construction of reality on the right and empiricism on the left. Traditionally, Western society has embraced the empirical view: that truth can be discovered and verified. Empiricism carries with it an enthusiastic belief in science and the principal product of science, empirically determined knowledge. Empiricism has dominated both the scientific view of the Western world and the lay view of what is true. We ask each other, 'Can you prove that?' and 'What data do you have?' Gradually, however, the newer research in many disciplines, such as physics, psychology, linguistics, sociology and recently cognition, is based in the social construction of reality. Or perhaps more accurately, empirically determined knowledge is understood by these disciplines as accurate within a given set of parameters which are themselves not verifiable by empirical means; that is, they are socially constructed.

The learning task related to empirical knowing (the left end of the continuum) is to discover the 'correct answer' and then to teach (communicate, influence) that answer to organizational members so that they can act accordingly. Empiricism necessitates the reduction of the whole into testable parts, leading to increased specialization. When organizations are firmly rooted in empiricism they see it as more important that certain specialized individuals learn the correct answer than that they collectively understand. The collective needs to know what to do but not necessarily why a certain course has been chosen.

The nature of reality and truth

Assumptions		Empirical knowing	Social construction of reality
Learning mode		Identify and learn from experts who have answers	Collectively create meaning

The nature of time

Assumptions	Learn then act	Act then learn	Learn through acting
Learning mode	Apply known principles	Reflect on actions and the consequences of those actions to derive principles	Design action so that it is possible to learn through the action

The nature of human nature

Assumptions		Theory X	Theory Y
Learning mode		Behaviour modification Reward and punishment	Development of new knowledge

The nature of human relationships

Assumptions		Individualism	Community
Learning mode		Improvement in the performance of each organizational member	Improvement in systemic processes

The relationship of the organization to the environment

Assumptions	Passive Recipient Victim	Exploiter Controller User	Symbiotic Enactment
Learning mode	Adaptive learning	Proactive learning	Co-construction of meaning

Information and communication

Assumptions		Systems structural	Interpretive
Learning mode		Accurate and widely distributed messages	Reduction in equivocality

Uniformity vs. diversity

Assumptions		Uniformity	Diversity
Learning mode		Wide acceptance of correct answers	Development of new knowledge; overcoming tacit assumptions

Nature of causality

Assumptions		Linear	Systemic
Learning mode		Scientific method Experimental design Single loop learning	Action research Naturalistic inquiry Action science Double loop learning

Figure 10.1   Organizational assumptions that facilitate organizational learning

The 'expert', whether external or internal, has significant influence in such organizations. This view is supportive of individual learning, but less so of collective learning.

At the other end of the continuum is the social construction of reality, a view that the reader will recognize as having been explicated throughout this book. It is built on the assumption that all knowledge is an interpretation, and is influenced by the cultural frame in which it is embedded. Further, all such interpretations are hypotheses to be continually tested and altered. The organizational learning task related to this assumption is the collective construction of meaning. Within this view learning would involve everyone, not just specialists, and it would be ongoing, since meaning structures are continually altered. As Schein (1992) notes in speaking to this set of assumptions, 'What must be avoided in the learning culture is the automatic assumption that wisdom and truth reside in any one source or method' (p. 366). The learning task is larger and more inclusive when the assumption is the social construction of reality.

The nature of time

There are three sequences of learning related to time:

1   Learn then act.
2   Act then learn.
3   Act through learning.

All three sequences are useful to organizations; however, it is the third that I have placed on the right on the continuum as most representative of organizational learning.

The 'Learn then act' model is the most familiar. When we think about organizational action we typically think about a sequence that involves first figuring out the correct way to proceed and then carrying out that solution. It is reminiscent of the school model where we learn first and then in our later years act. The actor's task, whether the actor is an individual member of an organization or a sub-unit of the organization, is to recall or find the correct principles or processes and then apply those to the situation. An example of this sequence might be an organization preparing to implement a quality effort which, before the effort begins, provides quality training courses for employees, or sends employees to visit other organizations which are successfully implementing quality programmes.

This is an effective model when two conditions exist: first, there is a known answer and secondly, the environment is relatively stable – that is, the environment in which the answer is applied is not greatly different from the one in which the knowledge was developed.

The 'Act then learn' model emphasizes reflection. It is a post-mortem approach in which those who have been involved in an action or project take the time to analyse systematically what has been learned from the experience. The questions organizational members ask themselves are 'What did we learn from doing that?' and 'How could we do it better next time?'. The goal is to derive principles or 'lessons learned' that can be used in a similar situation either by the same group or another part of the organization. The conditions under which the 'Act then learn' model is effective are when there are no known answers and when the environment is relatively stable and homogeneous so that the principles that are learned in one situation might be useful in another. The 'Act then learn' model is sometimes applied as an afterthought when it is discovered that, although the actors believed they had the right answer, it turned out to be wrong, and they need to know what went wrong so that they will not make the same mistake again. But it is probably most useful when it becomes a regular part of practice as the US Army's use of AARs and BP's completion meetings illustrate (see Chapter 6).

The third model is 'Act through learning', but it might just as accurately be labelled learn through acting. This is the integration of learning and acting rather than the separation suggested in the first two models. It may be difficult to think of learning and acting as concurrent because we are so used to thinking of learning as time out from action or even as an interference with action.

The learning tasks are those of self-correction, the invention of new knowledge and the creation of meaning. The question organizational members ask themselves is 'How can we design a way to learn in the process of carrying out this task?'. The conditions under which 'Act through learning' is effective are when the answer is unknown and when the environment is unstable and heterogeneous, so that every situation is unique. There is less time for the distribution of what has been learned in a fast-paced environment, so learning and acting must be concurrent and those who need the understanding derived from the learning must be involved in the action/learning rather than waiting for others to pass on their knowledge.

All three models of the relationship between learning and acting are useful, though each is most effective under the conditions ascribed to it. The conditions of the integrated model are those that are most congruent with the factors I have described as precipitating a new focus on organizational learning, that is, the organization is dealing with large amounts of equivocal information in an environment that is constantly changing, which gives rise to problems that the organization has never before addressed. Under such circumstances, rather than using known answers to solve problems, the organization must learn its way out of the problems it faces.

'Act through learning' requires that organizational members frame their interaction with the situation through a learning perspective. They start from a framework, which may be a best guess, and then, to use Schön's (1983) words, have a 'reflective conversation with the situation'. They attend to the result of the initial action, for example, how the action has altered the situation, or what other factors are now present. The altered situation may suggest a new action, one not even considered earlier. In fact, the organizational members may never have intended to go far down the first path, but only constructed an experiment to see what information the situation would yield as a result of the action. Schön says that to learn, organizational members must remain open to the situation's 'back talk'.

'Act through learning' requires up-front planning, but the planning is of a different nature from that needed for 'Learn then act'. In the latter, each step may be specified and sequenced in advance, and if necessary could be displayed in a graph or PERT chart. In the former, organizational members must plan carefully to determine what information would best inform their actions and how they might probe to call it forth. Thus in the latter the planning is for what organizational members should do and in the former for what they should learn. Ackoff (1981, p. 205) says, 'organizational learning occurs in response to immediate problems, imbalance, and difficulties more than it does in response to deliberate planning'. It is the intraorganizational conflicts and tension created by these immediate problems that lead to organizational learning.

The 'Learn then act' model is so pervasive, however, that even when answers are not known an organization may attempt to apply it. For example, the organization may demand detailed plans and specifics about cost and time lines in situations where no answer is apparent. When that happens an organizational member or unit who is charged with the responsibility for acting may feel it is necessary to act as if there were a known answer, even if there is not. Having committed to such a course the actor may then feel a need to hide any problems that arise if that answer does not work because not succeeding may be taken as evidence that the actor did not 'get it right' and that the organization needs to find someone who understands the situation better. The 'Learn then act' model allows greater management control than does either of the other two models, and for that reason may be more comfortable to management, who know they will themselves ultimately be held accountable.

The nature of human nature

This set of assumptions concerns the basic nature of human beings. Are human beings by nature passive and self-seeking or inquisitive and intent upon doing the best job they can? This is the assumption set explicated by McGregor (1960) as Theory X and Theory Y. After thirty years it would be hard to find a manager who would espouse Theory X, but less difficult to find managers whose behaviour belies their espousal of Theory Y. The problem managers have with achieving congruence on this issue illustrates how difficult it is for both individuals and organizations to alter their basic assumptions – even when they fully comprehend the benefits of doing so and are making a concerted effort to act in new ways.

If Theory X assumptions are made about human nature, then the most useful form of learning is that which is based on conditioning or behaviour modification. In such situations one group determines what it is necessary for another group to know. The learning issues are how to 'get' others to accept the sanctioned view and to carry out the sanctioned instructions. This view of learning was probably best expounded by Taylor (1915), who said:

Hardly a competent workman can be found who does not devote a considerable amount of time to studying just how slowly he can work and still convince his employer that he is going at a good pace. Under our system a worker is told just what he is to do and how he is to do it. Any improvement he makes upon the orders given to him is fatal to his success.

If, on the other hand, Theory Y is assumed, then the organization would expect its members to seek continually to make meaning of the events and actions that occur; that is, continually to develop new understanding. As we saw in Chapter 2, learning beyond simple conditioning requires the active participation of the learner. Learning is the internal process of making meaning, and is therefore not visible to others. It must then, of necessity, be voluntary and internally motivated if it is to occur at any level beyond simple conditioning.

The nature of human relationships

Human relationships can been seen as either individualistic or oriented toward the community. Kegan (1982) views this duality as the central issue of adult development. Kegan holds that human beings have deep yearnings for both agency and community and can resolve the dichotomy in favour of one over the other only temporarily; whichever side of the issue is in ascendancy, will, in the next stage of development, give way to the other.

Organizations have, however, clearly favoured individualism over community. Reward structures have been based on that assumption, as has the assignment of responsibilities and authority. It is only in the last decade that the more community-oriented concepts of teams and alignment around a vision have gained credence. The recent interest in organizational learning is perhaps also testimony to a new emphasis on community.

I have discussed the learning issues related to this assumption in greater depth in Chapter 8, and so will only summarize them here. If the organization accepts the view of individualism then learning would be conceived as improvement in individual skills and knowledge, and further that improved individual performance leads to improved organizational performance. Management development efforts would be aimed at individuals, even when offered in a class or group setting. Hiring and promotion would focus on competencies of individuals. Research would attempt to identify the characteristics of individuals that lead to organizational success.

The assumption that humans are oriented toward community would result in a focus on the learning of the collective. The questions would be less focused on individual competence and more focused on the collective processes – what happens in what Rummler and Brache (1990) call the 'white spaces' of the organizational chart. Clearly both types of learning are vital to organizations. It is, however, the latter which facilitates organizational learning.

The relationship of the organization to the environment

The term 'environment' generally implies a wide range of forces which influence the organization, for example, technological, economic and social changes, as well as larger systems, such as government, communities and the industry in which the organization is embedded as a sub-system. There are innumerable ways an organization could frame its relationship to the environment: for example, controller of, exploiter of, adaptive to, victim of, symbiotic with, explorer of. Each frame engenders a different stance toward organizational learning.

I place these assumptions about the environment into three broad categories: receptive, pro-active and co-determined. The type of organizational learning each is related to is suggested. The assumptions of the receptive category view the organization as the recipient of environmental forces and whims. The organization is seen as the object of environmental actions. The necessary learning tasks are, first, to be fully aware of what is happening through environmental scanning or other search processes, and, secondly, to make appropriate adaptations in response.

In the middle category the organization learns in order to control the environment or to exploit the opportunities the environment presents. As with the left-most position, this category views the organization as detached from the environment; the environment is an 'object' which can be analysed and understood in order to be controlled or acted upon. The organization is seen as capable of learning but the environment is not – therefore the environment should be acted upon rather than with. Learning processes might include scenario development, extensive market research and influence/negotiation strategies.

The right-most category views organizations as purposeful systems embedded in other purposeful systems (the environment) which are also capable of learning. It assumes a reciprocity between parts of the system in which each part can influence the others, necessitating that all parts of the system comprehend the other parts. It assumes that reality is, to a large extent, created rather than discovered. The learning task then is, jointly with other parts of the environment, to make sense of the total system and, again jointly, to co-create meaning and action based on that meaning. The organization 'enacts' the environment, meaning it is both acted upon and influences the environment.

Although we would expect organizational learning to result from all three categories of assumptions, how the organization plans and conducts its learning differs greatly among the three.

Information and communication

To frame this set of assumptions I will draw on the work of Daft and Huber (1987) who summarize two prevailing views of information and communication: the systems-structural perspective and the interpretive perspective.

The systems-structural perspective views information as messages and is therefore concerned with amount, frequency and distribution. Information is distributed within organizations for the purposes of deciding what action to take, to relay those decisions, to impart implementation information and to convey progress and results. The focus of learning is the receipt of accurate messages.

The interpretive perspective emphasizes the equivocality of information. This view is well articulated by Weick (1979): 'The manager literally wades into the swarm of "events" that surround him and actively tries to unrandomize them and impose some order' (p. 148). Thus, a given event may be interpreted in numerous different ways by organizational participants. In order for the organization to act the members must come to some agreed understanding of the meaning of the events. From the interpretive perspective, ambiguity precipitates an exchange of views rather than the collection of additional data.

Uniformity versus diversity

If learning is about identifying one right answer, then uniform agreement is to be prized. If, however, learning is the construction of meaning, then the more diversity available, the more likely both individuals and the collective are to escape the tacit assumptions that limit their understanding. As we saw in Chapter 3, diversity of perspectives is essential to the creation of new collective knowledge. But diversity is also essential to developing perspective on existing knowledge.

The nature of causality

The poles of this assumption are, on the one hand, that the world can best be explained by the cause and effect relationships that are related to linear thinking and on the other, that the world is complex and non-linear, and supposes multiple causality. The quality movement has made increased use of the linear view to make significant quality gains. Quality efforts are dependent upon the ability to identify cause and thereby to improve effect.

The complexity of the systemic view makes the use of experimental design to prove a cause and effect relationship less useful. If, as system theory suggests, all parts of a system are interrelated, so that to affect one part is to affect all of the others at some level, then the principle of holding all variables constant excepting that which is the subject of the experiment is not possible. The only hope of gaining a systemic view is, as Weisbord (1992) suggests, to get all the parties in the room at once.

Summary

If an organization intends to make maximum use of its learning capability then it is critical that the assumptions it makes about learning facilitate that direction. To do that the tacit assumptions that are a part of the collective meaning structure must again become a part of the accessible meaning structures of the organization so that they may be openly discussed and consciously chosen.

References

Ackoff, R. L. (1981). *Creating the Corporate Future*. New York: John Wiley and Sons.

Argyris, C., Putnam, R. and Smith, D. M. (1985). *Action Science*. San Francisco: Jossey-Bass.

Bellah, R. N., Madsen, R., Sullivan, W., Swidler, A. and Tipton, S. M. (1985). *Habits of the Heart*. Berkeley: University of California Press.

Daft, R. L. and Huber, G. P. (1987). 'How organizations learn: A communication framework'. *Research in the Sociology of Organizations*, **5**, 1–36.

Kegan, R. (1982). *The Evolving Self*. Cambridge MA: Harvard University Press.

McGregor, D. (1960). *The Human Side of the Enterprise*. New York: McGraw-Hill.

Rummler, G. A. and Brache, A. P. (1990). *Improving Performance: How to Manage the White Space on the Organization Chart*. San Francisco: Jossey-Bass.

Schein, E. H. (1992). *Organizational Culture and Leadership* (2nd edn). San Francisco: Jossey-Bass.

Schön, D. (1983). *The Reflective Practitioner*. New York: Basic Books.

Taylor, F. W. (1915). *The Principles of Scientific Management*. New York: Harper & Row.

Weick, K. (1979). *The Social Psychology of Organizing*. New York: Random House.

Weisbord, M. R. (1992). *Discovering Common Ground*. San Francisco: Berrett-Koehler.

Zuboff, S. (1982). 'New worlds of computer-mediated work'. *Harvard Business Review*, September/October, pp. 142–52.

11 Organizational learning and beyond

A tremendous amount of attention has been paid to organizational learning and knowledge management over the last five years, evidenced by the following:

- An ever growing number of organizations refer to themselves as 'learning organizations'. The words appear in annual reports, mission statements and the presentations of CEOs. I am not presuming that all who use these words have made the kinds of changes I have talked about in this book, but clearly the ideal is prized even when the reality may be lacking.
- Organizations are actively developing knowledge management processes such as knowledge databases, yellow pages that identify expertise in the organization, network meetings designed for knowledge sharing, teleconferencing systems that provide knowledge exchanges across units, and knowledge fairs (see Chapter 6). A 1997 (Kirby and Harvey) study of 431 organizations in the US and Europe found that 33 per cent had already developed knowledge repositories and another 24 per cent had plans in place to do so; 18 per cent

were mapping sources of internal expertise, with another 20 per cent with plans in place. There is an active and growing interest in finding ways to leverage existing organizational knowledge.

- Hundreds of large organizations have newly created positions of Chief Knowledge Officer (CKO) or Director of Organizational Learning. Stewart (1998) estimates that one-fifth of *Fortune 500* companies have someone in such a role. While I am not advocating the creation of such positions, I regard their appearance as a strong endorsement, by the top management of these organizations, of the role learning and knowledge play in their organization's success.

- Organizations are arranging and rearranging their physical space to make offices and factories more conducive to conversation and collaboration. Some of these efforts were described in Chapter 6 and Chaparral Steel's use of space was illustrated in Chapter 4. Although these new arrangements may have been instigated in order to save space or costs, regardless of the originating motivation the results are producing increases in the amount of sharing and collaboration in organizational settings.

- Many new processes have been developed that I would place in the category of 'whole system in the room', some of which were described in Chapter 6, e.g. Team Syntegrity, Future Search Conferences, Open Space Technology, Real Time Strategic Change, The Conference Model. The names of these processes do not have the word 'learning' or 'knowledge' in them, nor do the organizations that make use of these processes necessarily do so in order to implement organizational learning. Rather, such processes have become an important way to get the work of the organization done, e.g. develop a strategic plan, role out a new initiative, or resolve a critical problem. However, their basic design is rooted in the principles of collective learning and thus each time such a meeting is held the organization moves in the direction of organizational learning. When an organization holds Open Space or a Search Conference over a period of three days, it (a) generates information from all levels and units that is displayed around the room, (b) integrates that information through cross-functional meetings, (c) makes collective sense of what has been shared, and (d) involves local units in planning new actions based on that collective understanding. 'Whole system in the room' processes are an accelerated implementation of the organizational learning cycle.

- A variety of other new processes, described in this book, are aimed at getting the work of the organization done including Learning Maps, Appreciative Inquiry, and Action Learning. Again, what is significant about these new processes is that they are based on collective learning principles. I could, of course, enumerate other new processes that are not learning based, but my point is not that *all* new work processes are learning based, but that a remarkable number of them are. Moreover, the *variety* of learning-based work processes (Appreciative Inquiry is very different from Team Syntegrity) is growing as is the number of processes that are being used in organizations. It may well be that the future of organizational learning lies not in campaigns to convince everyone to be a learning organization, but in using what we know about collective learning to design more effective organizational processes.

- Organizations, regardless of the business they are in, are recognizing that they are a part of the knowledge economy. In the Kirby and Harvey (1997) study 87 per cent of the companies surveyed, labelled themselves as 'knowledge intensive'. These companies included a wide cross-section, e.g. manufacturing, banking, utilities, computers, health care, insurance, retail, transportation, oil and energy. The recognition of the role knowledge plays in an organization is the first step in figuring out how to leverage that knowledge. These numbers indicate that most organizations have taken that first step.

- There has been a growth in, and increasing sophistication of, collaborative software (e.g. group decision systems, conference systems) that allow organizational members to contribute to a decision, discussion, or the development of a document. The Kirby and Harvey study showed that 33 per cent of the companies surveyed had groupware in place and another 11 per cent had begun planning to put such systems in place. Again, these tools, although they do not carry a learning label, support the principles of organizational learning through their ability to integrate learning and develop a collective interpretation.

- Obvious to everyone has been the phenomenal growth of the Internet and intranets that make possible extended discussions on critical topics. These are discussions that everyone can take part in, often speaking more forthrightly over e-mail than they would have in person. There are fewer 'undiscussables' on an intranet than there are in a conference room. Getting 'undiscussables' into the organizational dialogue is critical to organizational learning.

- There is a growing acceptance of 'open-book management'; the idea that all organizational information is made available to everyone. When John Case wrote *Open-book Management* in 1995 he named a handful of companies that were experimenting with this idea – Springfield Re-Manufacturing being the much touted example. Case's second book published in 1998 is subtitled, *Lessons from over 100 companies who successfully transformed themselves*. This acceptance acknowledges that organizational members are *capable* of comprehending business data and that they can be of greater help in achieving agreed upon targets when they have full knowledge of what is happening.

The opening sentence of this chapter linked the two terms organizational learning and knowledge management. The examples cited here have been drawn from both categories and perhaps even more broadly. The labels used to describe this phenomenon keep evolving, e.g. organizational learning, learning organizations, intellectual capital, knowledge-based organizations, intelligent enterprise, knowledge management, learning capabilities. Some authors have made clear and often useful distinctions among these many labels. I certainly find some of the terms more meaningful and more descriptive than others. However, I have used them almost synonymously here because it seems that, even given their critical differences and unique origins, they are all a part of a growing recognition of the role that knowledge and learning play in organizational life.

I want to suggest they are all about something else as well. They are all about moving toward more democratic organizations. The movement toward organizational learning explicated above is, for the most part, intentional, while the movement toward more democratic organizations may be occurring as a by-product of that more purposeful effort. Because learning and governance are coupled, perhaps in ways most organizational members do not even recognize, learning inexorably leads to shared governance and shared governance requires learning.

The following examples illustrate this coupling. In the 1960s and 70s knowledge, even the practical knowledge of how to make something work better, was thought to be found in 'star cases' and 'leading edge examples'. The prevailing theory was that to get innovation you needed to put your best thinkers to work on a problem and after they had come up with answers, you diffused their work so that others could emulate what the experts had discovered. The question of the day was how to accomplish 'diffusion' and the studies were about 'early adopters' versus 'late adopters'. Our current thinking about how to solve difficult organizational problems is based more on give and take between *equal* partners. The idea of knowledge sharing is that every unit may be doing something that another unit could learn from. Ford provides a good example of this different emphasis (see Chapter 6). Although Ford calls its process 'Best Practice Replication' it is not about one plant being 'best,' rather it is an exchange among equals. Each of Ford's 26 Vehicle Operations Plants is presumed to have something to offer the other plants – and in fact, when the summary report for all 26 plants reveals that a particular plant has not contributed many new ideas, there is pressure on that plant to submit to the database – the idea is that everyone has something useful to offer. This change in how we think about innovation represents an increased respect for the knowledge of organizational members at all levels and a concomitant reduction in the reliance on an élite group of experts.

The Internet and groupware are also moving us toward more egalitarian exchanges. Sproull and Kiesler (1991) found that networked groups, whether through e-mail or real-time conferencing systems had more equal participation than face-to-face groups: 'Networks potentially permit broader access to information and more democratic structures than are now found in most organizations. Exploiting that potential will force managers to grapple with issues of responsibility and control' (p.116). I can see the difference in my own work at the university. Before e-mail, when an important issue crossed my desk, I might, as programme director, have checked with a colleague or two in nearby offices. With e-mail I am much more likely to send a quick message to get the thoughts of all the faculty on a decision or idea. Moreover, the responses are sent to everyone, so that everyone has access to everyone else's thinking, rather than their ideas being filtered through only my perceptions. The access to valid information is fundamental to shared authority and the increased access that electronic networks provide is making that more possible.

As stated above, 'whole system in the room' processes are based on the principles of organizational learning and I will add that they are based in the principles of democracy. They bring together people from all levels of the organization to learn with and from each other. The assumption is that knowledge is dispersed, thus the whole organization (or representatives of it) must be in the room in order for what the organization 'knows' to be present. In such meetings all ideas are displayed around the room so that everyone has access to what everyone else is discussing. No organizational member or class of members is privileged by having their words accorded special attention either in writing or in speeches. Weisbord (1992) quotes Angus, Frank and Rehm: 'We believe the real world is knowable to ordinary people and their knowledge can be collectively and meaningfully organized. In fact, ordinary people are an extraordinary source of information about the real world' (p. 13). This is basically a democratic belief. A belief in democracy rather than the aristocracy of a knowledgeable few. A belief that people are collectively capable.

Open-book management, another example from the list above, is about access to information, a fundamental principle of democracy. Open-book management is based on the idea that everyone has a right to have available the critical information of the organization. Moreover, there is the belief that organizational members are capable of understanding and using the complex information of the organization. Thomas Jefferson (1820) said: 'I know of no safe depository of the ultimate powers of the society but the people themselves, and if we think them not enlightened enough to exercise their control with a wholesome discretion, the remedy is not to take it from them, but to inform their discretion'. Organizations that have implemented open-book management often find that they must help members learn the language and concepts of business in order for them to contribute as partners in the organization's work – 'they must inform their discretion'.

It is understandable that organizational learning would be connected to more democratic forms of governance. 'Knowledge is power' is a truism few of us would question. When knowledge is concentrated at the top, the top has power. When knowledge is diffuse, so then is power. It is because of this strong connection between knowledge and power that I am concerned about how organizational members are thinking about their responsibilities (see Chapter 9). Knowledge is surely becoming more diffuse, moving to organizational members and out of the concentrated hands of a few. But organizational members must be prepared to use this knowledge and its concomitant power wisely. It is hoped that that wisdom can be generated out of the dialogue of organizational members.

There is a fear we hold about organizations becoming more democratic, a fear that organizational members will make mistakes – poor decisions. But the risk of mistakes exists in all forms of governance including our current form of governance in organizations in which the power is concentrated at the top. None of us would have any trouble identifying numerous recent mistakes organizations have made – from laying off large numbers of people only to hire them back again, to rolling out a change plan that no one understood or could use. Moreover, the opportunity to make mistakes is the opportunity to learn. Just as paternalism in lives prevents the development of our own abilities and judgement, so organizational paternalism prevents an organization from developing its knowledge and capabilities.

It is, I believe, possible to begin to implement organizational learning without an accompanying move toward shared authority, but it is not possible to move far in that direction. As many of the organizations that have moved the farthest with organizational learning can affirm, they soon find themselves faced with the issues of power, equity and governance. Learning and action are connected in the brains of human beings.

Organizational members cannot make responsible choices if they do not know what is going on; when they find themselves working without adequate knowledge, over time, they tend to become apathetic or self-serving. Conversely, when organizational members have made collective sense of organizational issues but are not allowed to act on that understanding, they become frustrated and angry. Hence the frustration of many who have spent hours working on a task force only to have their recommendations ignored or never implemented (Dixon, 1997). By nature we are creatures who need knowledge in order to act and who need to act on what we know. Charles Handy (1989) speaks of this in *The Age of Unreason*: 'It is tempting to impose our goals on other people . . . We may get our way, but we don't get their learning. They may have to comply, but they will not change. We have pushed out their goals with ours and stolen their purposes. It is a pernicious form of theft which kills the will to learn' (p. 74).

When I use the word 'democracy', what comes to mind for many people is voting. However, I am not talking about voting here but something that is much more complex. Democracy is about freedom of speech, freedom of assembly, access to information, choice of who we place in authority positions, a way to dismiss those in authority without bloodshed, the right to benefit from one's own labours, and the protection of individuals against abuse and injustice. These are the 'rights' that we prize in our public life and that are for the most part missing from our organizational life. I am not the first to note the incongruity between our public and organizational governance. However, we have become so accustomed to living in a democracy and, for the most part, working within a totalitarian régime, that we can hardly envision any other possibility. Granted the totalitarian leadership is often benevolent and sometimes we are even among the favoured who benefit from the totalitarian régime.

I spoke about one side of this incongruity in Chapter 9 where it was suggested that organizational members had some responsibilities to the organization as a whole which they were not living up to but which were required of them if the organization was to learn. Here I want to suggest that the whole has some responsibilities to organizational members that make organizational learning more workable. These are the rights of democracy given above and restated for organizations:

- Organizational members have full access to organizational (business) information.
- Organizational members participate in the self-management of local units.
- Organizational members participate in the design of the larger system.
- People in authority positions have accountability to those who report to them. That accountability includes:
  - organizational members having a voice in the decisions about who is placed in authority positions over them
  - organizational members having an ordered way to dismiss people in authority positions when they are not serving those who report to them well.
- Organizational members benefit directly from unit and organizational successes.
- Organizational members have a voice in the changes that impact them.
- The establishment of an independent entity to protect these rights.

Organizational learning requires responsibilities of organizational members beyond compliance and the accomplishment of an assigned task. It requires of them that they contribute their ideas, share their knowledge, and that they engage in a proactive search for better ways to do things. In other words, that they act in the interest of the whole. This requirement to be responsible to something larger than self, demands a concomitant stake in the ownership of that larger entity. This is the essence of democracy, a widely distributed sense of ownership and responsibility. My belief is that organizational learning is moving us in the direction of more democratic organizations. And it may even be that, if we construct more democratic organizations, they would greatly improve our collective ability to learn.

References

Case, J. (1995). *Open-book Management*. New York: HarperBusiness.

Case, J. (1998). *The Open-book Experience: Lessons From Over 100 Companies who Successfully Transformed Themselves*. Reading, MA: Addison Wesley.

Dixon, N. M. (1997). 'Action Learning: More than Just a Task Force', in M. Pedler (ed.), *Action Learning in Practice* (3rd edn). Gower, pp. 329–38.

Handy, C. (1989). *The Age of Unreason*. Harvard Business School Press.

Jefferson, T. (28 September 1820).

Kirby, J. and Harvey, D. (1997). 'Executive perspectives on knowledge in the organization.' Center for Business Innovation, E&Y.

Sproull, L. and Kiesler, S. (1991). 'Computers, networks and work'. *Scientific American*, September, 116–23.

Stewart, T.A. (1998). 'Is this job really necessary?' *Fortune*, 12 January.

Weisbord, M.R. and 35 International Co-authors (1992). *Discovering Common Ground*. San Francisco: Berrett-Koehler.

Appendix A: Definitions of organizational learning

It may be helpful to contrast the definition of organizational learning that I have used in this book with other definitions in the literature. I have provided eleven definitions here, listed in the reverse order of their year of publication, starting with the definition I have used in this book in order to provide the comparison.

- Organizational learning is the intentional use of learning processes at the individual, group and system level to continuously transform the organization in a direction that is increasingly satisfying to its stakeholders. (Dixon, 1994)
- A learning organization is one that consciously manages its learning processes through an inquiry-driven orientation among all its members. (Kim, D. 1992. 'Systemic quality management: improving the quality of doing and thinking'. *Systems Thinker*, **2** (7), 1–4)
- A Learning Company is an organization that facilitates the learning of all its members and continuously transforms itself. (Pedler, M., Burgoyne, J. and Boydell, T. 1991. *The Learning Company*. New York: McGraw-Hill)

- ... organizations where people continually expand their capacity to create the results they truly desire, where new and expansive patterns of thinking are nurtured, where collective aspiration is set free, and where people are continually learning how to learn together. (Senge, P. 1990. *The Fifth Discipline.* New York: Doubleday)
- ... institutional learning, which is the process whereby management teams change their shared mental models of their company, their markets, and their competitors. (De Geus, S. P. 1988. 'Planning as learning'. *Harvard Business Review,* March/April, 70–4)
- ... new knowledge is manifested in new structural arrangements, new culture, and new collective action. (Normann, R. 1985. 'Developing capabilities for organizational learning', in J. M. Pennings et al. (eds), *Organizational Strategy and Change.* San Francisco: Jossey-Bass)
- Organizational learning means the process of improving actions through better knowledge and understanding. (Fiol, C. M. and Lyles, M. A. 1985. 'Organizational learning'. *Academy of Management Review,* **10** (4), 803–13)
- Organizational learning is defined as the process by which knowledge about action outcome relationships between the organization and the environment is developed. (Daft, R. L. and Weick, K. E. 1984. 'Toward a model of organizations as interpretation systems'. *Academy of Management Review,* **9** (2), 284–95)
- Learning results from the adaptive and manipulative interactions between an organization and its environments. (Hedberg, B. 1981. 'How organizations learn and unlearn', in P. Nystrom and W. Starbuck (eds), *Handbook of Organizational Design.* New York: Oxford University Press)
- Organizational learning includes both the processes by which organizations adjust themselves defensively to reality and the processes by which knowledge is used offensively to improve the fits between organizations and their environments. (Hedberg, B. 1981. 'How organizations learn and unlearn', in P. Nystrom and W. Starbuck (eds), *Handbook of Organizational Design.* New York: Oxford University Press)

- Organizational learning is a process in which members of an organization detect error or anomaly and correct it by restructuring organizational theory of action, embedding the results of their inquiry in organizational maps and images (Argyris, C. and Schon, D. A. 1978. *Organizational Learning: A Theory of Action Perspective.* Reading MA: Addison-Wesley)

The definitions offer a great variety of possible meanings for the term 'organizational learning'. Some of the more notable differences among the definitions include:

- A focus on the organization's relationship to the external environment versus a more internal focus.
- A focus on adaptation versus a proactive stance of creating a desired future.
- The learning of individuals versus a focus on the learning of larger organizational units, such as the team or total system.
- Management as the major player in organizational learning versus a broader view that includes members at all levels of the organization.
- A focus on taking action versus a focus on the organization's underlying assumptions.

In spite of the variety and confusion engendered by this diversity of meanings, there also appear to be common themes in some if not all of the definitions:

- *The expectation that increased knowledge will improve action.* Many of the definitions imply that there is a causal relationship between the quality of knowledge that employees have and the effectiveness of an organization's actions. Quality of knowledge may relate to *more* information and *more accurate* information, as well as *more widely shared* information.
- *An acknowledgement of the pivotal relationship between the organization and the environment.* Taking an open systems view, many of the definitions reference the environment as

the major element about which the organization must learn and to which the organization must adapt or manipulate.

- *The idea of solidarity, as in collective or shared thinking.* Central to several of the definitions is the idea that organization members have in common shared assumptions or understandings. These shared understandings may need to be uncovered, corrected or expanded to facilitate effective organization action.
- *A proactive stance in terms of the organization changing itself.* Many of the definitions imply that through learning, the organization is able to self-correct in response to environmental change or to transform itself in anticipation of a desired future.

Appendix B: Glossary

Accessible meaning structures	That part of the individual's cognitive map which he or she makes available to others in the organization.
Actions	Verbal or non-verbal responses that are mediated by meaning structures.
Automatic response	An individual's response which is based on a tacit meaning structure. The individual does not need to 'think' in order to respond, as in the return of a greeting.
Chunking	The mental act of placing data into larger categories in order to relate the larger 'chunks' to each other.
Cognitive map	The network of the meaning structures of the individual which constitute what an individual knows or understands.

Collective interpretation	Interaction among organizational members in order to reduce the equivocality of information.
Collective meaning structures	That part of the individual's cognitive map which is held jointly by virtually all members of the organization.
Data	Awareness of sense data or data from instruments, which are extensions of our senses.
Defensive routines	Tacit organizational practices that are developed in order to reduce embarrassment, save face, or lessen conflict, but in so doing limit both individual and collective learning.
Dissonance	An experience of internal discomfort resulting from information that conflicts with the individual's existing meaning structures.
Equivocal information	A given event is subject to different interpretations by organizational participants.
Espoused theories	The way we explain our actions to ourselves and others. Espoused theories are frequently in contradiction to our theories-in-use.
Explicit meaning structure	Meaning structure of which the individual is aware, that is, it is in conscious awareness.
Long-term memory	A metaphorical space where the meaning structures composed in working memory are stored and from which they are retrieved.

Meaning structure The organisation of experience that is constructed in working memory and stored in the long-term memory of the individual. There are many names for this concept, among them, schema (Bartlett, F. C. (1932). *Remembering*. Cambridge, UK: Cambridge University Press), and meaning scheme (Mezirow, J. (1991). *Transformative Dimensions of Adult Learning*. San Francisco: Jossey-Bass).

Meta-cognition An individual's knowledge of his or her own cognitive processes.

Organizational dialogue Interaction in a collective setting that results in mutual learning upon which the organization can act.

Organizational learning The intentional use of learning processes at the individual, group and system level to continuously transform the organization in a direction that is increasingly satisfying to its stakeholders.

Private meaning structures That part of individuals' cognitive map which they choose not to make accessible to others in the organization.

Situated learning Learning that occurs in the context of work itself, both in terms of the work space and timing.

Spaced learning Learning that is spaced over months rather than compressed into sequential days.

Tacit comprehension activity The unintentional mental activity of individuals that is outside of their conscious awareness but which nevertheless leads to the formulation or reformulation of meaning structures.

Tacit meaning structures   Meaning structures that are lost to individuals' conscious awareness through familiarity.

Theories-in-use   Tacit meaning structures, formulated as if–then propositions. Theories-in-use mediate action and are often in contradiction to an individual's espoused theories.

Working memory   A metaphorical space in which the processing of information takes place; where new information is related to the individual's meaning structures from long-term memory.

Index

abuse 225
accessible meaning 46–8
accountability 225
'act then learn' model 206
'act through learning' model 206–8
action learning 170–71
actions 33, 162–3
    causal relationships 163
    influence of meaning structures 29–31
    measurement 162–3
active experimentation 41
agreement 115
ambiguous information 38, 53, 169, 212
analysis of information 4, 5
answers 2, 5, 54–5
Appreciative Inquiry (technique) 219
Argyris, Chris 14–15, 40
assertions 110, 115
assumptions 54, 116–20, 199–203, 214
authority to take action 63, 120–22, 125,
    128, 194–5, 222, 225
    see also power
autonomy 142, 145–6, 150, 191
awareness 54

Bateson, Gregory 14, 40

Bechtel (company) 144
behaviours 5, 16, 26, 29, 33, 34, 111, 160,
    169
benchmarking 73, 177
Best Practice Replication Process (Ford)
    163
British Petroleum (company) 131–2,
    143, 149
business literacy 135, 220

causal relationships in processes 155–6,
    158, 161, 163, 164, 213
Center for Creative Leadership 179–80
change 1, 3, 6, 8, 83, 84, 87–90, 105,
    169–70, 187, 191, 224, 225
    relationship with learning 2–4
Chaparral Steel (company) 68–76
Chesapeake Packaging Company 142–3
Chevron (company) 132–3, 135
chunking of data 31–2
co-participation in an organization 191
cognition 14, 20, 37, 52, 114–15, 203
    meta-cognition 37–8
cognitive map (concept) 20–21
collaboration in learning 174–5
collaborative software 219

collective interpretation of information
55, 103–9, 112, 118, 120, 125, 127–8,
141–2
collective learning 14, 52–7, 59, 61, 63,
64, 93–122, 138, 146, 150, 174–5,
188, 205, 213, 218
commitment to 194
see also organizational learning
collective meaning 47, 48–50, 58, 214
Commercial Casework (company) 134
common space in offices 60–61, 109
communication 9, 19, 25, 36, 56, 83, 212
lateral communication 192
see also dialogue; organizational
dialogue
compensation *see* reward systems
competence 110, 113, 175, 210
competition 6, 83, 138
competitive advantage 45
comprehension 7, 19, 20, 25, 26, 34, 114
see also understanding
conceptual conflict 113
conceptualization 66, 102
concrete experience (concept) 40
consent (to authority) 195
continuous collection of information 97
continuous transformation (in
organizations) 8
control 5, 58
courage 190
criticism 34
cross-functional teams 185–6
cultural information 26
customer needs 6

dashboard measures (concept) 147–8,
151
data 16, 17–8, 22, 27, 28, 34, 36, 47–8, 51,
55–6, 65, 80, 96, 152, 155, 161, 165,
174, 177, 212, 220
chunking of data 31–2
incomplete 26
interpretation 17–26, 63, 91
participant generated 55–6
see also databases; information
databases 129–30, 130–31, 133, 134, 135,
217–18
decentralization 143
decision making 5, 9, 26, 58, 126, 128,
131, 141–6, 152, 168, 170, 194–5,
219
by groups 58
delegation 9, 143
democracy 221, 223, 224–5
Dewey, John 39
diagnoses of situations in work 4
dialogue 51, 105, 107, 110–16, 140–41
organizational 110–16, 188–9, 196
see also information; organizational
dialogue
differences 16–17, 53, 95–6
disconfirming evidence 27
discussions *see* dialogue
disequilibrium 113
dissemination of information 8, 101,
126–36, 151
dissonance (sense of) 29, 36, 113, 175
diversity of perspectives 213

egalitarianism 52–3, 70, 76, 105–9, 222
empiricism 203
enactment (concept) 3
environmental factors affecting
organizations 211–12
equality in relationships 106–7, 108
equifinality (concept) 2
errors 27, 110, 111–13
see also mistakes
expectations 16, 40
experiences 15, 30–31, 40, 41, 128, 157,
160, 170, 175, 186–7, 193–4
experiential learning cycle (Kolb) 65
experimentation 8, 41, 66, 193
expertise 44, 73, 105–6, 129, 171–2,
203–4, 218, 222
see also knowledge
experts 171–2, 203–5
explicit meaning structures 34, 35
external information 93–7, 98–103

facilitating factors for learning 156–8
federalism in companies 143
Ford (company) 135, 136
freedom to speak openly 106
Freire, Paulo 40, 107
funnel approach to information
interpretation 105

Gagné, Robert 14
General Electric (company) 140
generation of information 63–4, 74,
   93–8, 125–8, 147, 172, 218–19

goals 5, 73, 84, 117, 118, 142, 159, 176,
   186, 188, 189, 202, 224
governance of organizations 194–5, 221,
   223, 225
group decision making 58
groupware 219–20, 222

hallway conversations 46–7, 50–57, 59,
   140–41
   common space in offices 60–61
Hewlett Packard (company) 134
hierarchies 46, 52–3, 108–9, 194, 197
   see also organizations – structure
human nature as a factor in
   organizational culture 202, 208–9
humility in relationships 107
hypothesis testing 115–16

ideas 6, 47, 49, 52, 53, 56, 59, 60–61, 69,
   71–2, 73, 93, 95, 108, 110, 113, 116,
   130, 138, 144, 160, 175, 185, 186, 196,
   222, 226
   diversity in 95
imagination 27
incomplete data 26
individual development 13–41, 43, 38–9,
   57, 59–60, 95, 111
individualism 199–200, 210
inferences 4, 36–7, 159
information 4, 5, 7, 10, 13, 15–17, 22, 25,
   27, 29, 35, 36, 38, 45, 40, 53, 61,
   63–8, 70, 74–6, 82, 84, 85, 90, 96,
   99–100, 105, 110–12, 114, 118, 121,
   122, 148, 172, 175, 186, 190, 207, 212,
   218–19, 225
   access to 223, 225
   analysis of information 4, 5, 135
   ambiguous 38, 53, 169, 212
   collective interpretation 103–9, 112,
      118, 120, 125, 127–8, 141–2
   continuous collection of information
      97
   cultural information 26
   dissemination 8, 101, 102, 126–36, 151

effects of specialization 102
external information 93–7, 98–103
funnel approach to information
   interpretation 105
generation of 63–4, 74, 93–8, 125–8,
   147, 172, 218–19
infrastructure considerations 125–52
intangible information 192
internal information 74, 94, 97–8,
   98–103
oral summarizing 51–2, 115
synthesis of 4
verbal transmission 15
withholding 111–12
   see also collective interpretation of
      information; data; databases;
      dialogue; interpretation of
      meaning; knowledge; meaning
      – structures; messages
information technology 5, 129
infrastructure for organizational
   learning 125–52
ingenuity 144
injustice 225
innovation 6, 71, 72, 73, 97–8, 143, 221
intangible information 192
intellective skills (concept) 6, 10
interdependence in federal companies
   143–4
internal information 74, 94–5, 97–8,
   98–103
Internet 220, 222
interpersonal skills 32–3
   see also relationships
interpretation of meaning 4, 17–26,
   63–4, 65–6, 103–4
interpretive perspective on information
   and communication 63, 212
intranets 220

Johnsonville Foods 82–90, 148
judgment 5, 6, 224
   see also decision making

Kao Corporation 101
knowledge 3, 5, 7, 19, 20, 25, 28, 33, 41,
   44, 52, 61, 69, 70–74, 87, 105, 114,
   120, 121, 128–9, 136–7, 144, 158–61,

164, 168, 183, 185, 187, 189–90, 203,
    207, 213, 218, 222–3, 224, 226
  changes in 158–61
  measurement 159–61
  shared knowledge 130, 131, 132,
    135–6, 155, 192, 221
Knowledge Age (concept) 1, 4
knowledge management 217
Knowles, Malcolm 40, 108
Kolb, David 40

language 20, 25, 191
lateral communication 192
LeaderLab (Center for Creative
    Leadership) 179–80
leadership 1
'learn then act' model 205–6, 208
learning 1–10, 43–61, 106, 116–20, 148–9,
    155, 168–9, 173, 211
  action learning 170–71
  by managers 167–81
  collaboration 174–5
  commitment to 193–4
  cycle of 63–90, 126–8
  defined 7, 227
  individual 38–9, 41, 59–60
  need for 38–9
  planning for learning 208
  relationship with change 2–4
  relationship with truth 27–8
  relationship with work 5–6
  situation learning 170–71, 186
  spaced learning 173
  theoretical framework 13–41
  see also collective learning;
    organizational learning
learning maps 140, 219
Lewin, Kurt 39
linear thinking 213
local autonomy 142
long-term memory 19–20, 22, 25, 34, 36,
    103

Management By Objectives 186
managers 4, 138, 167–8, 196
  development for organizational
    learning 167–81
Manco (company) 134–5
Mead, George Herbert 41

meaning 6, 7, 14, 15, 17–26, 40–41, 47,
    53, 54, 56, 59, 95, 103–4, 107,
    114–15, 175, 207, 212
  accessible 46–8
  collective 47, 48–50, 58, 214
  diversity 96
  explicit 34, 35
  interpretation of 4, 17–26, 63–4, 65–6
  private 44–6
  structures 17–18, 19–21, 26–31, 36, 38,
    40, 43–4, 49, 59, 63, 100, 105, 107,
    110, 199
  tacit 32–6, 49
  see also collective meaning
measurement of knowledge 159–61
measurement of organizational learning
    155–66
measurement of results 146–52
meetings 56–7, 111, 131, 136, 139
  informal 61
  see also dialogue
memory 20, 31–7
  see also long-term memory; working
    memory
messages 31
  delaying 100
  modification 100
  routing 100
  summarizing 100
  see also communication; information
meta-cognition 14, 37–8
Mezirow, Jack 40
mistakes 6, 72, 94, 111–13, 146–7, 150,
    170, 206, 223, 224
  see also errors
motivation 209
multiple perspectives 53–4
multi-skilling 70–71, 74–5, 103
Mumford, Alan 40

nature of work 4–6
networking 222
  see also Internet; intranets
non-linear thinking 213
non-verbal meaning 20
Northern Telecom (company) 177–8
Norway Emerging Areas (BP
    subsidiary) 151

objectives *see* goals
'on-the-job' learning *see* situation
  learning
'open book management' 220, 223
organizational culture for learning
  199–214
organizational dialogue 110–16, 187,
  188–9, 196, 223
  see also dialogue
organizational learning 1–10, 43–61, 87
  cultural factors 199–214
  cycle of 63–90, 126–8
  defined 6–10, 227–30
  effects of size 109
  future prospects 217–26
  in hallways 50–57
  infrastructure 125–52
  measurement 155–66
  responsibilities of staff 183–97, 226
  size of firms (as a factor in
    organizational learning) 109,
    145
  theoretical framework 93–122
  time factors 205–8
  see also collective learning
organizations 1–10, 43–61, 63–90, 107–8,
  142–3, 145, 183–5, 189–90, 192–7,
  219
  co-participation in an organization
    191
  culture for learning 199–214
  defined 8–9
  environmental factors 211–12
  governance 194–5
  structure 39, 88, 125–52
  see also organizational learning
outcomes in organizational
    performance 54, 88–90, 144, 155–6,
    164, 189–90
  unpredictable outcomes 57

Pace Industries (company) 135
participant generated data 55–6
patterns (in human interactions) 27
Peer Assist (BP system) 131–2, 135
performance management 85, 194
personal computers 4
  see also information technology
perspectives 53–4, 110, 113–14, 186

diversity of 213
Piaget, Jean 39
planning for learning 208
power 143, 183, 190, 223
  distribution of 187
private meaning 44–6
problem solving 54–5, 69–70, 171–2, 207
'problem-then-theory' approach 171,
  172
Published Image Inc. (company) 143

questions 53

reality 202
  nature of 203–5
reasoning 110, 114–15, 172, 174
reflection (of experiences) 171, 175, 193,
  206
reflective observation (concept) 40, 66
relationships 25, 27, 95, 106–8, 126, 168
  as a factor in organizational culture
    202
  humility in 107
  nature of 210
  respect in relationships 106, 107
repositories of knowledge 217
respect (concept) 107
responsibilities of staff in organizational
    learning 112, 172, 183–97, 223, 226
Revans, Reg 40
reverse delegation 143
reviewing results 146–52
reward systems 86, 144–6
risk taking 72, 122
Royal Dutch Shell (company) 143

San Diego State University 178
selection processes 16, 86–7
self-actualization 38
self-correction 8
self-fulfilling prophecies 27, 36
self-managed work teams 142
self-perception 33
Self-Q interview (technique) 161
shared experience 56–7
shared knowledge 130, 131, 132, 135–6,
  150–51, 192
shared responsibilty 95
shared understanding 99

short-term memory 19
situation learning (in real work) 168,
    170–71, 177, 186
size of firms (as a factor in
    organizational learning) 109, 145
space as a factor in organizational
    culture 202
spaced learning 173
speaking as a form of learning 51–2
Sprint (company) 134
Stayer, Ralph 83
subsidiarity in companies 143
subversion 121
success 67, 87, 94, 103, 144, 145, 150, 225
superstitious learning (concept) 163
supporting evidence 27
syntax 25
synthesis of information 4
systems-structural perspective on
    information and communication
    212
systems theory 96

tacit assumptions 54
tacit meaning structures 32–6, 49
tacit organizational assumptions 54,
    116–20
Team Syntegrity (group thinking
    technique) 138–9, 219
teamwork 5, 30, 31, 88, 162, 165–6
technological change 3
    see also innovation
'theory-then-application' approach 171,
    172
Theory X behaviour 209
Theory Y behaviour 209

time as a factor in organizational
    culture 202, 205–8
time factors in management
    development 173
totalitarian leadership 225
training 72
truth 14, 27–8, 202
    nature of 203–5

unawareness 54
uncertainty 112–13
understanding 7, 8, 19, 20, 27, 28, 38, 52,
    55, 58, 99, 120, 159, 174, 175, 187,
    207
uniformity of perspective 213
Unilever (company) 143
unpredictable outcomes 57
US Army 133 (knowledge sharing)
    133–4, 148, 149

values 138, 201, 202
verbal transmission of information 15
video-conferencing 132
voicing perspectives 113–14
Volvo Truck Management programme
    178–9

'whole system in the room' processes
    136–7, 152, 218, 222
withholding of information/knowledge
    111–12, 190
work (nature of) 4–6
working memory 19–20, 22, 31–7, 59
    see also memory
WorkOut problem solving technique
    140
World Health Organization 76–82